© by:

Search The Scriptures Ministries

www.searchthescripturesministries.org

The Bible Teaching Ministry

of

Mark Allen Deakins
Contact Phone: (423) 321-2990

Preface

Before we begin this study on "The Lordship of Christ" we must understand the necessity of such a study. In our churches we have done a fairly decent job of presenting the "Salvation Message" of the Gospel of Jesus Christ. There are more "Salvation Roads" then I would care to count. The most notable one is probably "The Roman Road to Salvation." It would appear something like …

1. The Problem of Sin
   Romans 3:23: "For all have sinned and come short of the glory of God.
2. The Punishment of Sin
   Romans 6:23: "For the wages of sin is death; …"
3. The Payment for Sin
   Romans 5:8: "But God commended His love toward us; in that while we were yet sinners, Christ died or us."
4. The Path of Salvation
   Romans 10:17: "So then faith comes by hearing, and hearing by the word of God."
5. The Profession of Salvation
   Romans 10:9-10: "That if thou shall confess with your mouth the Lord Jesus, and shall believe in your heart that God has raised Him from the dead, you shall be saved. For with the heart man believes unto righteousness; and with the mouth confession is made unto salvation."
6. The Plea for Salvation
   Romans 10:13: "For whosoever shall call upon the name of the Lord shall be saved."
7. The Passion of Salvation
   Romans 10:11: "For the scripture says: Whosoever believes on Jesus shall not be ashamed."

The confession of individual Christians and Churches is that "Jesus is our Savior and Lord." But in truth I believe that an honest confession would have to be that "Jesus is our Savior." Somewhere we have lost the concept that Jesus is to be our LORD and KING, and not just our Savior. It is time for The Church and individual Christians to reaffirm The Lordship of Christ in our lives. This Study will aim to present the different aspects of Jesus Christ's Lordship and how these should affect our lives. So – We begin our study of The ABC's of The Lordship of Christ as found in the Book of Hebrews.

Note: The Format of this Study will be as follows:
First an Alliterated Outline of the Section of Scripture
Next will follow a simple exegesis of the Scripture.

TABLE OF CONTENTS

Intro. v. 1:1-3: The Acceptance of The Lordship of Christ	1
I. v. 1:4-13: The Abiding Name of The Lordship of Christ	3
II. v. 1:14 – 2:5: The Belief of The Lordship of Christ	9
III. v. 2:6-11: The Central Focus of The Lordship of Christ	12
IV. v. 2:12-18: The Development of The Lordship of Christ	15
V. v. 3:1-11: The Example of The Lordship of Christ	21
VI. v. 3:12-19: The Forewarning of The Lordship of Christ	24
VII. v. 4:1-11: The Gospel of The Lordship of Christ	28
VIII. v. 4:12-16: The Holy Bible of The Lordship of Christ	36
IX. v. 5:1-11: The Inspiration of The Lordship of Christ	41
X. v. 5:12 – 6:8: The Journey to The Lordship of Christ	46
XI. v. 6:9-12: The Kindling of The Lordship of Christ	56

XII. v. 6:13-20: The Lively Hope of The Lordship of Christ	65
XIII. v. 7:1-10: The Money Involvement of The Lordship of Christ	70
XIV. v. 7:11-28: The New Order of The Lordship of Christ	77
XV. v. 8:1-13: The Operation of the New Order of The Lordship of Christ	81
XVI. v. 9:1-15: The Purification in The Lordship of Christ	86
XVII. v. 9:16-28: The Quantification of The Lordship of Christ	95
XVIII. v. 10:1-18: The Remission of Sins in The Lordship of Christ	99

XIX. v. 10:19-25: The Sanctuary (Congregational)
  Worship in The Lordship of Christ
  <u>Intro. The Beginning of Sanctuary Worship
     v. 19-21</u>
	102

XIX. v. 10:19-25: The Sanctuary (Congregational)
  Worship in The Lordship of Christ
  <u>1. The Beliefs of The Believers
     v. 22a</u>
	104

XIX. v. 10:19-25: The Sanctuary (Congregational)
  Worship in The Lordship of Christ
  <u>2. The Belonging of Believers
     v. 22b</u>
	111

XIX. v. 10:19-25: The Sanctuary (Congregational) Worship in The Lordship of Christ <u>3. The Boldness of Believers</u> <u>v. 23</u>	120
XIX. v. 10:19-25: The Sanctuary (Congregational) Worship in The Lordship of Christ <u>4. The Bond of Believers</u> <u>v. 24a</u>	128
XIX. v. 10:19-25: The Sanctuary (Congregational) Worship in The Lordship of Christ <u>5. The Bolstering of Believers</u> <u>v. 24b</u>	141
XIX. v. 10:19-25: The Sanctuary (Congregational) Worship in The Lordship of Christ <u>6. The Brotherhood of Believers</u> <u>v. 25a</u>	153
XIX. v. 10:19-25: The Sanctuary (Congregational) Worship in The Lordship of Christ <u>7. The Building-Up of Believers</u> <u>v. 25b</u>	160
XX. v. 10:26-39: The Training of The Lordship of Christ	166
XXI. v. 11:1 – 12:4: The Unequivocal Following of The Lordship of Christ	174
XXII. v. 12:5-17: The Validation of The Lordship of Christ	181
XXIII. v. 12:18-29: The Worship Places of The Lordship of Christ	188

XXIV. v. 13:1-6:	The X-pectations of The Lordship of Christ	194
XXV. v. 13:7-17:	The Yard-Lines of The Lordship of Christ	201
XXVI. v. 13:18-21:	The Zone of The Lordship of Christ	209
XXVII. v. 13:22-25:	The ABC of The Lordship of Christ	212

**Intro. v. 1:1-3: The ACCEPTANCE of
The Lordship of Christ**
  A. v. 1: Sovereign Lead Prophets
     "God …spoke … to the fathers by the prophets"
    1. Different Times
      "Who at various times "
    2. Divers Manners
      "and in various ways"
    3. Distant Past
      "spoke in time past"
  B. v. 2-3a: Son of Promise
     "has in these last days spoken to us by His Son …"
    1. Chosen
      "whom He has appointed heir of all things"
    2. Creator
      "through whom also He made the worlds"
    3. Celestial
      "who being the brightness of His glory"
  C. v. 3b-f: Sign {express image} of Permanence
    1. Person
      "of His Person {God}
    2. Power
      "and upholding all things by the word of His power"
    3. Purging
      "when He had by Himself purged our sins"
    *. Place
      "sat down at the right hand of the Majesty on high"

Intro. v. 1:1-3: The ACCEPTANCE
              of The Lordship of Christ
    Before we can begin a study of the Lordship of Christ and apply what we learn to our lives and to the life of the Church we must first "accept the claim that Christ is to be our Lord." We can understand this by understanding How the Eternal God has chosen to reveal Himself to mankind.

A. v. 1: Sovereign Led Prophets

We have been informed that in the past that God chose to speak to our forefathers by the prophets. God did this at various times and in various ways. In the Old Testament we find that many times a prophet of God would show up "on the scene" at the most unexpected times. God also used different methods to deliver His message: such as signs, miracles, dreams, and so forth.

B. v. 2-3a: Son of Promise

Now in "these last days" God has chosen to speak to mankind by His Son. This being God's choice requires man to accept Christ's Lordship. For Christ is "heir of all things." All things belong to Christ. Not only do all things belong to Christ as a gift from the Father but all things belong to Christ because "through Him all things were created." God, the Father, has chosen to allow His glory to be shown through Jesus Christ.

C. v. 3b-f: Sign {express image} of Permanence

Jesus also has the claim of Lordship over us because He is God {the express image of His (God, the Father) Person}. By nature of His Godhood He keeps everything in our universe working in their proper order. He also is the one whom has "by Himself purged our sins" when we accept His offer of salvation through His shed blood on the cross. After Jesus completed His work of salvation he has "sat down at the right hand of the Majesty on high" signifying that His work has been completed.

Therefore we can accept Jesus' claim of Lordship over our lives.

**I. v. 1:4-13: The ABIDING NAME of
       The Lordship of Christ**
v. 4: "having become so much better than the angels, as He has by inheritance obtained a more excellent name than they."

  A. v. 5-7: Permanent Condition
    1. v. 5: Will of The Almighty
"For to which of the angels did He {The Father} ever say: *"You are My Son, Today I have begotten You"?* and again: *"I will be to Him a Father, And He will be to me a Son"?*
    2. v. 6: Worship of Angels
"But when He again brings the firstborn into the world, He says: *"Let all the angels of God worship Him."*
    3. v. 7: Witness of Angelic
"And of the angels He says: *"Who makes His angels spirits And His ministers a flame of fire."*

  B. v. 8-9: Pure Character
    1. v. 8a: His Ruler-ship
"But to the Son He says: *"Your throne, O God, is forever and ever:"*
    2. v. 8b-9a: His Righteousness
"But to the Son He says: *"… A scepter of righteousness is the Scepter of Your kingdom. You have loved righteousness and hated lawlessness;"*
    3. v. 9b: His Rejoicing
"But to the Son He says: *"… Therefore God, Your God, has anointed You with the oil of gladness more than Your companions."*

  C. v. 10-13: Power of Creation by Comparison
   1. v. 10: Creator vs. Created
    "But to the Son He says: "*… You, Lord, in the beginning laid the foundation of the earth. And the heavens are the work of Your hands.*"
   2. v. 11: Continuer vs. Cast Off
    "But to the Son He says: "*… They will perish, but You remain; And they will all grow old like a garment;*"
   3. v. 12: Ceaseless vs. Changed
    "But to the Son He says: "*… Like a cloak You will fold them up, and they will be changed. But You are the same, and Your years will not fail.*"
   *. v. 13: Chosen vs. Conquered
    "But to which of the angels has He ever said: "*Sit at My right hand, till I make Your enemies Your footstool.*"

■■■

I. v. 1:4-13: The Abiding Name of
    The Lordship of Christ
  Once one has ACCEPTED the Lordship of Christ then the study of Christ's Lordship becomes a meaningful endeavor. The first thing that one must accept regarding the Lordship of Christ is His Abiding Nature. Verse four of this section of Scripture gives us the key to understanding Christ's Abiding Nature.
  A. v. 5-7: Permanent Condition
   Verse 4 begins with "having become so much better than the angels" referring to Christ's Lordship. Then verse 5 informs us that His Lordship is The Will of the Almighty God; for God said to Jesus: "You are My Son, Today I have begotten You." It is the will of the Father that Jesus be glorified as His only Son. Jesus has been placed above all because of the Father's will. Verse 6 and 7 inform us of the worship and witness and the angels in heaven concerning Christ's Lordship. All angelic beings understand the place that Jesus Christ has been given by the Father.

B. v. 8-9: Pure Character
>
> The middle part of verse 4 reads "as He has by inheritance" referring to the fact that Jesus Christ by nature is one that has a pure character. God, the Father, says to Jesus: "Your throne, O God, is forever and ever." Jesus has the natural right to rule because even God, the Father, calls Him "God." Because Jesus is God He is also perfect. When He came and lived a life as "a man" He was in all ways tempted as we are, yet without sin. His righteousness gives Him the right to be our Lord. By making Christ our Lord we will become partakers of the "gladness" that is found in pleasing the Father.

C. v. 10-13: Power of Creation by Comparison
>
> Finally verse 4 tells us that Jesus has "obtained a more excellent name than the angels." His Lordship will last forever because He is the ...
>> Creator, not the created
>> Continuer, not the cast-off
>> Ceaseless One, not to be changed
>
> and He is the ...
>> Chosen One that will conquer all.
>
> "Therefore God also has highly exalted Jesus Christ and given Him the name which is above every name. That at the name of Jesus every knee should bow, of those in heaven, and of those on earth, and of those under the earth and that every tongue should confess that Jesus Christ is Lord, to the glory of God the Father" (Philippians 2:9-11).

*. The Abiding Name of the Lordship of Christ
>
> The whole Bible is filled with references to Jesus in one way or another. Beyond that, the primary message spread by the Lord Himself and his followers was that everyone needs to go directly to Jesus Himself, place a submissive-obedient faith and trust in him and continue to the end of salvation. It is very easy to see why we are directed by God to do this after noting the various ways the Lord Jesus is described by His many names

and titles. Each refers to yet another important place or position that Jesus holds in God's plan for man's salvation. Please ponder how precious and preeminently important Jesus is for man's salvation. The truth is: Jesus is the all-sufficient Savior. No other savior is needed besides Him or with Him. (Notice that this is just a partial listing of the many Scriptural names and titles of the Lore Jesus Christ. Many others are not listed here.)

    Advocate (1 John 2:1)
    Almighty (Rev. 1:8; Mt. 28:18)
    Alpha and Omega (Rev. 1:8; 22:13)
    Amen (Rev. 3:14)
    Apostle of our Profession (Heb. 3:1)
    Atoning Sacrifice for our Sins (1 John 2:2)
    Author of Life (Acts 3:15)
    Author and Finisher of our Faith (Heb. 12:2)
    Author of Salvation (Heb. 2:10)
    Beginning and End (Rev. 22:13)
    Blessed and Only Ruler (1 Tim. 6:15)
    Bread of God (John 6:33)
    Bread of Life (John 6:35; 6:48)
    Bridegroom (Mt. 9:15)
    Capstone (Acts 4:11; 1 Pet. 2:7)
    Chief Cornerstone (Eph. 2:20)
    Chief Shepherd (1 Pet. 5:4)
    Christ (1 John 2:22)
    Creator (John 1:3)
    Deliverer (Rom. 11:26)
    Eternal Life (1 John 1:2; 5:20)
    Faithful and True (Rev. 29:11)
    Faithful Witness (Rev. 1:5)
    Faithful and True Witness (Rev. 3:14)
    First and Last (Rev. 1:17; 2:8; 22:13)
    Firstborn From the Dead (Rev. 1:5)
    Firstborn over all Creation (Col. 1:15)
    Gate (John 10:9)

God (John 1:1; 20:28; Heb. 1:8; Rom. 9:5;
    2 Pet. 1:1; 1 John 5:20 & ect.)
Good shepherd (John 10:11,14)
Great Shepherd (Heb. 13:20)
Great High Priest (Heb. 4:14)
Head of the Church (Eph. 1:22; 4:15; 5:23)
Heir of all things (Heb. 1:2)
High Priest (Heb. 2:17)
Holy and True (Rev. 3:7)
Holy One (Acts 3:14)
Hope (1 Tim. 1:1)
Horn of Salvation (Luke 1:69)
I Am (John 8:58)
Image of God (2 Cor. 4:4)
Immanuel (Mt. 1:23)
Judge of the living and the dead (Acts 10:42)
King Eternal (1 Tim. 1:17)
King of Israel (John 1:49)
King of the Jews (Mt. 27:11)
King of kings (1 Tim. 6:15; Rev. 19:16)
King of the Ages (Rev. 15:3)
Lamb (Rev. 13:8)
Lamb of God (John 1:29)
Lamb Without Blemish (1 Pet. 1:19)
Last Adam (1 Cor. 15:45)
Life (John 14:6; Col. 3:4)
Light of the World (John 8:12)
Lion of the Tribe of Judah (Rev. 5:5)
Living One (Rev. 1:18)
Living Stone (1 Pet. 2:4)
Lord (2 Pet. 2:20)
Lord of All (Acts 10:36)
Lord of Glory (1 Cor. 2:8)
Lord of lords (Rev. 19:16)
Man from Heaven (1 Cor. 15:48)
Master (Lk. 5:5; 8:24; 9:33)
Mediator of the New covenant (Heb. 9:15)
Mighty God (Isa. 9:6)

Morning Star (Rev. 22:16)
Offspring of David (Rev. 22:16)
Only Begotten Son of God (John 1:18; 1 John 4:9)
Our Great god and Savior (Titus 2:13)
Our Holiness (1 Cor. 1:30)
Our Husband (2 Cor. 11:2)
Our Protection (2 Thess. 3:3)
Our Redemption (1 Cor. 11:2)
Our Sacrificed Passover Lamb (1 Cor. 5:7)
Power of God (1 Cor. 1:24)
Precious Cornerstone (1 Pet. 2:6)
Prophet (Acts 3:22)
Rabbi (Mt. 26:25)
Resurrection and Life (John 11:25)
Righteous Branch (Jer. 23:5)
Righteous One (Acts 7:52; 1 John 2:1)
Rock (1 Cor. 10:4)
Root of David (Rev. 5:5; 22:16)
Ruler of God's Creation (Rev. 3:14)
Ruler of the Kings of the Earth (Rev. 1:5)
Savior (Eph. 5:23; Titus 1:4; 3:6; 2 Pet. 2:20)
Son of David (Lk. 18:39)
Son of Man (Mt. 8:20)
Son of the Most High God (Lk. 1:32)
Source of Eternal Salvation (Heb. 5:9)
The One Mediator (1 Tim. 2:5)
The Stone the builders rejected (Acts 4:11)
True Bread (John 6:32)
True Light (John 1:9)
True vine (John 15:1)
Truth (John 1:14; 14:6)
Way (John 14:6)
Wisdom of God (1 Cor. 1:24)
Word (John 1:1)
Word of God (Rev. 19:13)

"For it is written: "As I live, says the Lord, Every knee shall bow to Me and every tongue shall confess to God." (Romans 14:11).

II. v. 1:14 – 2:5: The BELIEF of
The Lordship of Christ

A. v. 1:14 – 2:2: Shared Scripture
  1. v. 14: Heirs of Salvation
     "Are they not all ministering spirits sent forth to minister for those who will inherit salvation?"
  2. v. 1: Heeding The Scripture
     "Therefore we must give the more earnest heed to the things we have heard, lest we drift away."
  3. v. 2: Heart-Felt Steadfastness
     "For if the word spoken through angels proved steadfast, and every transgression and disobedience receive a just reward,"
B. v. 3-4a: So Great Salvation
     "how shall we escape if we neglect so great a salvation"
  1. Son
     "which at the first began to be spoken by the Lord"
  2. Sharers
     "and was confirmed to us by those who heard Him"
  3. Source
     "God also bearing witness"
C. v. 4b-5: Special Sharing
     "witness … according to His own will"
  1. Signs
     "with signs"
  2. Spectacular
     "and wonders, with various miracles"
  3. Spirit
     "and gifts of the Holy Spirit"
  *. v. 5: Subject – To Christ [implied]
     "For He has not put the world to come, of which we speak, in subjection to angels."

II. v. 1:14 – 2:5: The Belief of
The Lordship of Christ
When we consider the Lordship of Christ we must by necessity consider our Basic Core Beliefs and what those Beliefs are based upon. The foundation for the Lordship of Christ in our lives is …

A. v. 1:14 – 2:2: Shared Scriptures
It is the Holy Scriptures that we learn about Christ and the salvation that He offers. "… you have known the Holy Scriptures, which are able to make you wise for salvation through faith which is in Christ Jesus." After becoming heirs of salvation by accepting Christ as Savior we then can understand that "all Scripture is given by inspiration of God, and is profitable" if we heed its teachings. By following the Bible's teachings with all our hearts we will find that "as children of God we will be complete, thoroughly equipped for every good work." (2 Timothy 3:15-17).

B. v. 2:3-4a: So Great Salvation
The great question here is "How shall we escape if we neglect so great a salvation?" In truth this is a rhetorical question. If an individual rejects this salvation that is offered through the Son of God {Jesus Christ} and refuses to share the blessings that is offered by the Source of salvation {God, the Father} then that one will not escape the punishment that awaits. John was given a vision of that punishment and spoke of it: "I saw a great white throne and Him who sat on it, from whose face the earth and the heaven fled away. And there was found no place for them. And I say the dead, small and great standing before God, and the books were opened. And another book was opened, which was the Book of Life. And the dead were judged according to their works, by the things which were written in the books. … Then Death and Hades were cast into the lake of fire. This is the second death. And

       anyone not found written in the Bok of Life was cast into the lake of fire" (Revelation 20:11-15).
C. v. 4b-5: Special Sharing

    The thing is, "God desires all men to be saved and to come to the knowledge of the truth. For there is one God and one Mediator between God and men, the Man Christ Jesus." (1 Timothy 2:4-5). God would have everyone to accept the signs and spectacular events that prove that Jesus Christ is His Son and would have all to receive the salvation offered in Christ through the power of the indwelling Spirit. Even so God has chosen to allow man to have free will and to reject His calling if they so choose. With this known mankind must also understand that all things have been placed under Christ and He will be the judge of the world at the end.

    Our Basic Core Beliefs as Christians should compel us to accept the Lordship of Christ in our lives.

III. v. 2:6-11: The CENTRAL-FOCUS of
The Lordship of Christ

A. v. 6-7a: Concern Over Man – "What is man?
  1. Mindful of Man
     "you are mindful of him"
  2. v. 6c: Meeting of Man
     "or the Son of man that You take care of him?"
  3. v. 7a: Making of Man
     "you have made him a little lower than the angels"

B. v. 2:7b-8: Crown of Man
   "You have crowned him with glory and honor"
  1. v. 7c: Domain
     "and set him over the works of Your hands"
  2. v. 8a: Dominion
     "You have put all things in subjection under his feet"
  3. v. 8b: Dominance
     "For in that He put all in subjection under him, He left nothing that in not put under him."

C. v. 2:9-11: Coronation of Christ {The God-Man)
   v. 9a-b: "we see Jesus … crowned with glory and honor"
  1. v. 9c: Ability to Die
  2. v. 10: Acceptance of Death
     "For it was fitting for Him, for whom all things and by whom are all things, in bringing many sons to glory, to make the captain of their salvation perfect through sufferings."
  3. v. 11a: All-Inclusiveness of Deliverance
     "For both He who sanctifies and those who are being sanctified are all on one"
  *. v. 11b: Adoption of the Devoted
     "for which reason He is not ashamed to call them brethren."

III. v. 2:6-11: The Central-Focus of
   The Lordship of Christ
   Now that we understand the foundation for the core belief of the Lordship of Christ we must look at the Focus of Christ's Lordship.
   A. v. 6-7a: Concern Over Man
      We are asked to consider "What is man that God is mindful of him?" We see that God is mindful of man in that we can "cast our cares upon Him for He cares for us." The text which says that "God has made man a little lower than the angels" is a quote from Psalm 8:5. But we must understand that in Psalm 8:5 the actual Hebrew wording is God had made man "a little lower than *Elohim*" = *Elohim* {God}. In Genesis 1:27 we are told that "God created man in His own image, in the image of God He created him, male and female He created them." God is mindful of man because we are the glory of God's creation.
   B. v. 2:7b-8: Crown of Man
      God crowned man with glory and honor in that He has set His creation under the dominion of man. Although we have been given the task of "tending" God's world we must never forget that this world was created for man's use. Some would "exchange the truth of God for the lie, and worship and serve the creature or creation rather than the Creator, who is blessed forever." (Romans 1:25). It is true that because of the sinful fall of man that mankind has given up much of his dominion, we are still the central focus of God's creation.

C. v. 2:9-11: Coronation of Christ {The Man-God}

Because mankind is the central-focus of The Lordship of Christ, God sent Jesus into the world that we as a race could find forgiveness of sins and renew a right relationship with Him through Christ. This was accomplished when Jesus came into the world and took upon Himself a human body. This was necessary to give Jesus {God} the ability to die for the sins of man. Jesus also accepted this role for us as our redeemer by accepting death, even death upon the cross. The Gospel of Christ {His death, burial, and resurrection from the dead} was done that "whosoever believes on Him should not perish, but have everlasting life." (John 3:16). "But as many as receive Him, to them He gave the right to become children of God, even to those who believe in His name." (John 1:12).

IV. v. 2:12-18: The DEVELOPMENT of
The Lordship of Christ

Intro. v. 11: "He is not ashamed to call them brethren"
   v. 12a: "I will declare Your name to My brethren;"

A. v. 2:12b-13: The Adoption in Christ
   1. v. 12b: into the Church
      "In the midst of the assembly I will sing praise to You"
         Colossians 1:18: "And Jesus is the head of the body, the Church."
   2. v. 13a: by Christ – Trust in Him
      "I will put My trust in Him"
      Romans 10:9-13: "that if you confess with your mouth the Lord Jesus and believe in your heart that God has raised Him from the dead, you will be saved.
         For with the heart one believes unto righteousness, and with the mouth confession is made unto salvation.
         For the Scripture says, Whoever believes on Him will not be ashamed.
         For there is no distinction between Jew and Greek, for the same Lord over all is rich to all who call upon Him.
         For whoever calls on the name of the Lord shall be saved."
   3. v. 13b: as Children
      "Here am I and the children whom God has given Me"
      John 1:12-14: But as many as received Him, to them He gave the right to become children of God, to those who believe in His name:
         Which were born, not of blood, nor of the will of the flesh, nor of the of man, but of God.
         And the Word became flesh and dwelt among us, and we beheld His glory, the glory as of the only begotten of the Father full of grace and truth."

B. v. 14-16: The Authority in Christ
    v. 14a: Flesh and Blood - Life
1. v. 14b: Father of Death
1 John 4:4: "You are of God, little children, and have overcome them, because He who is in you is greater than he who is in the world."
2. v. 15: Fear of Death
1 Corinthians 15:54-57: "Then shall be brought to pass the saying that is written: Death is swallowed up in victory.

O Death, where is your sting? O Hades, where is your victory?

The sting of death is sin, and the strength of sin is the law.

But thanks be to God, who gives us the victory through our Lord Jesus Christ."
3. v. 16: Fact of Death
John 11:25-26: "Jesus said to her, I am the resurrection and the life. He who believes in Me, though he may die, he shall live.

And whoever lives and believes in Me shall never die. Do you believe this?"

C. v. 17-18: The Atonement in Christ = High Priest
1. Gracious = "merciful"
"Destination of faith"
    Heb. 12:1 = "race set before us"
2. Guaranteeing = "faithful"
"Author of faith"
    Heb. 12:2
3. Guarding = "propitiation"
"Finisher of faith"
    Heb. 12:2
*. v. 18: Giver of Aid
    Heb. 12:3: For consider Him who endured such hostility from sinners against Himself, lest you become weary and discouraged in your souls."

IV. v. 2:12-18: the Development of
   The Lordship of Christ
      Realizing that we as a race and as individuals are the central focus of The Lordship of Christ we might ask how this Lordship can be developed in a person's life? We see this development when we are told of Jesus: v. 11: "He is not ashamed to call them brethren" and that Jesus (v. 12) "will declare Your (God's) name to My brethren." This Lordship of Christ will begin developing in …
  A. v. 2:12b-13: The Adoption in Christ
    1. v. 12b: into the Church
         This adoption is first of all "into the Body of The Church for "in the midst of the assembly I will sing praise to You." The assembly refers to the congregational fellowship that Christians find in the "Body of Christ." In Colossians 1:18 we are told that "Jesus is the head of the body, the Church." If an individual is going to fellowship with Jesus that one must fellowship with Jesus through His body. This can only be done through the fellowship of the local Church Body {Jesus' Body}. It may be true that one can worship God anywhere [admitting that most will not do so]; but to fellowship with Christ one must do so through the fellowship with the local Church Body. One cannot separate fellowship with Christ from fellowship with the Local Church.
    2. v. 13a: By Christ – Trust in Him
         The only way one can have a right relationship with God is through a right relationship with Jesus Christ. Over and over in the New Testament we are informed that there is no other way of salvation. Christianity is an exclusive faith. Jesus Himself said: "I Am The Way, The Truth, and The Life. No man can come to the Father except by Me."

3. v. 13b: as Children
      Jesus said: "Here am I and the children whom God has given Me." Every Christians begins the spiritual journey as a "spiritual baby." We are told that as spiritual children we should desire the "sincere milk of the Word of God that we can grow thereby." We are told to "grow in the grace and knowledge of our Lord Jesus Christ." We are commanded to "grow up into Christ in everything."
B. v. 14-16: The Authority in Christ
      We are told that Jesus became a partaker of flesh and blood. We understand from John 1:14 that the "Word {Jesus} became flesh and dwelt among us, and we beheld His glory, the glory as of the only begotten of the Father, full of grace and truth." As children of God through Christ we are to live in the authority (Lordship) of Christ because He took on life that we might be able to defeat all the aspects of death that we might face.
   1. v. 14b: Father of Death – Defeated
      "You are of God, little children, and have overcome them, because He who is in you is greater than he who is in the world." (1 John 4:4). We are given the ability in Christ to overcome the world because of the power of Christ that is within us. For whoever is born of God overcomes the world. And this is the victory that has overcome the world—our faith. Who is he who overcomes the world, but he who believes that Jesus is the Son of God." (1 John 5:4-5).
   2. v. 15: Fear of Death – Destroyed
      After one has accepted Christ as Savior and Lord "then shall be brought to pass the saying that is written: Death is swallowed up in victory. O Death, where is your sting? O Hades (the grave), where is your victory? the sting of death is sin, and the strength of sin is the law. But thanks be to God, who gives us the victory through our Lord Jesus Christ." (1 Corinthians 15:54-57).

3. v. 16: Fact of Death – Diminished

Having Jesus as one's Lord changes one's perceptions about death. Jesus said: "I am the resurrection and the life. He who believes in Me, though he may die, he shall live. And whoever lives and believes in Me shall never die. Do you believe this?" Because Jesus is our Lord we will never truly die. These bodies of ours may see corruption but our souls will never die for "to be absent from the body is to be present with the Lord."

C. v. 17-18: The Atonement in Christ = High Priest

In Hebrews 12:1-3 we are encouraged to understand that Jesus was incarnated (took upon Himself flesh and blood) like us that He might be …

1. Gracious = "merciful"

Jesus is gracious in that He has given us a destination of our faith. He has encouraged us to "lay aside every weight, and the sin which so easily ensnares us, and let us run with endurance the race that is set before us." Jesus' mercy is seen in us when we are forgiven for the sin which so often invades our lives. He then helps us to understand that we have not "already attained, or reached perfection, but are to press on, that we might lay hold of that for which Christ Jesus has also laid hold of us. We do not count ourselves to have apprehended; but one thing we do, forgetting those things which are behind and reaching forward to those things which are ahead, we press toward the goal for the prize of the upward call of God in Christ Jesus." (Philippians 3:12-14).

2. Guaranteeing = "faithful"

Jesus is "the author of our faith." "For by grace you have been saved through faith, and that not of yourselves; it is the gift of God, not of works, lest anyone should boast. For we are His workmanship, created in Christ Jesus for good works, which God prepared beforehand that we should walk in them." (Ephesians 2:8-10). We can "be confident of this very

thing, that He {Jesus} who has begun a good work in you will complete it until the day of Jesus Christ." (Philippians 1:6).
3. Guarding = "propitiation"

Not only is Jesus the author of our faith He is also "the finisher of our faith." Jesus, being our Great High Priest, makes "propitiation for the sins of the people." It is Jesus Himself that "reconciles" us to God. "For this reason I am willing to suffer many things; nevertheless I am not ashamed, for I know whom I have believed and am persuaded that He is able to keep what I have committed to Him until that Day." (2 Timothy 1:12).

*. Giver of Aid

"For in that he Himself has suffered, being tempted, yet without sin, He is able to aid those who are tempted." "For consider Him who endured such hostility from sinners against Himself, let you become weary and discouraged in your souls." (Hebrews 12:3). Because Jesus has experienced everything that we have experienced we have reason to know that He can and will come to our aid in times of need. Henceforth, "let us not grow weary while doing good, for in due season we shall reap if we do not lose heart. Therefore, as we have opportunity, let us do good to all, especially to those who are of the household of faith." (Galatians 6:9-10).

V. v. 3:1-11: The EXAMPLE of
The Lordship of Christ
- A. v. 1b-4: Consider The Lord Jesus Christ
  1. Position of Christ
     a. v. 1b: The Apostle of our Confession
     b. The High Priest of our Confession
  2. v. 2-3a: Prominence of Christ
     a. Faithful
     b. Counted Worthy of More Glory
  3. v. 3b-4: Products of Christ
     a. He is greater than the Creation (House = Cosmos)
     b. He is the Creator
- B. v. 5-6: Confidence in The Lord Jesus Christ
  1. Servant's Example
     "and Moses indeed was faithful in all his house as a servant, for a testimony of those things which would be spoken afterward"
  2. Son's Encouragement
     "but Christ as a Son over His own house, whose house we are if we hold fast the confidence"
  3. Spirit of Expectation
     "and the rejoicing of the hope firm to the end"
- C. v. 1a & 7-11: Consecration to The Lord Jesus Christ
  1. v. 1a & 7: Heavenly Calling of Faith
     a. Partakers of the Heavenly Calling
     b. Perception = "hear the voice of the Spirit"
  2. v. 8-9: Heartfelt Course to Follow
     a. Soft Hearted = "not hardened in rebellion"
     b. Spiritual Sight = "see God's works"
  3. v. 10: Hurtful Condition to Fear
     a. Disloyal Attitudes = "hearts that go astray"
     b. Disobedient Actions = "not know God's ways"

*. v. 11: Horrifying Circumstance to Flee
   a. Wrath of God– "It is a fearful thing to fall into the hands of the living God." (Hebrews 10:31).
   b. Wrongful Worship of God –
      – "Create in me a clean heart, O God; and renew a right spirit within me. Cast me not away from thy presence; … Restore unto me the joy of thy salvation; …" (Psalm 51:11-12).

■■

V. v. 3:1-11: The Example of
          The Lordship of Christ
   Here we are given an example of how we are to respond to the Lordship of Christ. The example is threefold in consideration: (1) Our High Priest - Jesus, (2) The Helper – Moses, and (3) The Horrible – The Children of Israel.
 A. v. 1b-4: Consider The Lord Jesus Christ
   Jesus is the greatest example that we could consider in any situation. First we must understand that Jesus was given two positions: He is the Apostle of our confession and He is the High Priest of our confession. As the apostle of our confession He is the one that has presented God's offer of salvation to mankind. Jesus represents the Father to us. As the High Priest of our confession He represents us to the Father. By accepting Jesus blood as a covering for our sin we have the righteousness of Christ imputed to us that we may appear before the Father as clean and pure. The Prominence of Jesus is seen in the fact that He is faithful to the One (God) who has appointed Him as Apostle and High Priest. Jesus has completely fulfilled the Father's requirements of payment for sin when He died on the cross. Jesus also must be considered as "the Creator of all things: "all things were made through Him, and without Him nothing was made that was made." (John 1:3). The Creator is always greater than the creation.

B. v. 5-6: Confidence in the Lord Jesus Christ
    Remembering that the Book of Hebrews was written first to the Jewish Nation we can understand the example that Paul gives concerning Moses. Moses was a faithful servant, but his service was to the things that belonged to another {to God}. Jesus, on the other hand, was faithful in His service but His service concerned "His own house, who house we are if we hold fast the confidence." Many of the Jews were devoted to Moses and the law more than they were devoted to God Himself. We are encouraged to find joy and hope in The Son of God not only in the servant of God.

C. v. 1a, 7-11: Consecration to The Lord Jesus Christ
    We have been given a "heavenly calling" of faith in the Lord Jesus Christ. We have been directed to consider "if we will hear His voice." Jesus said: "My sheep hear my voice, and I know them, and they follow me." The longer individuals have been born again the easier it should be for them to "recognize" the voice of Jesus when He speaks to their hearts through the Person of the indwelling Holy Spirit. As God speaks to us we must be careful that we "do not harden our hearts as in the rebellion, in the day of trial in the wilderness." This wilderness experience was when the children of Israel refused to enter into the Land of Promise. They allowed fear to keep them from obeying God's direct instructions. We are to have spiritual sight and look for and distinguish the works of God in our lives. He concludes this section of Scripture with a stern warning not to let our "hearts go astray and not know God's ways." If we choose to be disobedient we will not enter into the rest of God. Remember that "it is a fearful thing to fall into the hands of the living God." (Hebrews 10:31). We should seek to worship God properly by praying to God: "Create in me; a clean heart, O God; and renew a right spirit within me. Cast me not away from thy presence; … Restore unto me the joy of thy salvation; …" (Psalm 51:11-12).

VI. v. 3:12-19: The Forewarning of The Lordship of Christ

  *. Beware Brethren …

  A. v. 12: Suspicious Heart
  "an evil heart of unbelief"
  1. Doubts God –
   – "Did God really say …?"
  2. Disputes God's Word –
   – "What God really meant was …"
  3. Departs from the living God –
   – "heap to themselves teachers, having itching ears"

  B. v. 13: Stony Heart
  "hardened through the deceitfulness of sin
  1. Dirty Actions –
   – "God gave them over to uncleanness"
  2. Despicable Affections –
   – "God gave them over to vile affections"
  3. Degenerate Acceptability –
   – "God gave them over to a reprobate mind"

  C. v. 15: Stubborn Heart
  "Do not harden you hearts as in the rebellion"
  1. Self Centered –
   – "everyone did what was right in their own eyes"
  2. Social Conscience –
   – "think they will be seen of men"
  3. Spiritual Contamination –
   – "they did not retain God in their memory"

  *. Sequential Consequences –
   – "So we see that they could not enter in because of unbelief

VI. v. 3:12-19: The Forewarning of
            The Lordship .of Christ
"Beware Brethren …" is how this portion of Scripture begins. As the children of God born anew by the blood of Christ and filled with the presence of the Holy Spirit we must always be alert to allowing our hearts to be defiled by the constant interaction with a sinful world. This passage of Scripture warns about three conditions that can affect the heart of the Brethren, if not guarded against, and causing the believers to reject the Lordship of Christ.

A. v. 12: Suspicious Heart

First we are warned "lest there be in any of you an evil heart of unbelief in departing from the living God." We can see the progress of unbelief in a believer's heart by the tactic used by the devil when he spoke with Eve. The first thing that the devil did was to bring up doubts concerning God's Word – "Did God really say …?" "Is the Bible really the inspired Word of God or just a collection of books penned by men that have no real spiritual value?" These are the questions that the devil uses to bring about doubt concerning the Word of God. This is the first step downward leading to a heart of unbelief. The next step is shrouded so as not to seem a direct attack on God: "Yes God said …; but what does God really mean?" Or something like: "We know what God meant when the Scriptures were written but this is a new age and surely the Scriptures mean something different today." Disputing God's Word is now called Academic Criticism. Many now believe that the Bible cannot mean what it says: therefore it must mean something else. This second step then leads to those that depart from the living God in that "they heap to themselves teachers, having itching ears." They like the "form of preaching" but not the substance of the preached Gospel of Christ. We see this in the many "speakers of today." Notice, I do not call them "preachers" because the truth is that they are not preaching the Gospel of Christ but preachers of a different gospel and should be accursed before God. (Galatians 1:8).

B. v. 13: Stony Heart

We are warned not to be "hardened through the deceitfulness of sin." There is an old saying about sin which goes something like this:

> Sin will keep you longer than you mean to stay,
> Sin will cost you more than you meant to pay,
> Sin will take you further than you meant to go,

In Romans 1 we find a description of the downward progression of someone that allows the "deceitfulness of sin" to harden their heart. The first thing that will begin to affect someone is when they begin to justify "dirty actions" in their life. If these actions are continued we are told that "God will give them over to uncleanness." Once this happens then an individual will begin to have "despicable affections" as "God gives them over to vile affections." After one has begun to defend dirty actions and allowed themselves to justify despicable affections that individual will harden their heart to the point where they have "degenerate acceptability." At this point "God will give them over to a reprobate mind." God says of these individuals that "their way shall be unto them as slippery *ways* in the darkness: they shall be driven on, and fall therein: for I will bring evil upon them, *even* the year of their visitation." (Jeremiah 23:12).

C. v. 15: Stubborn Heart

Again we are warned not to be like the children of Israel when they refused to enter into the rest of their Lord by entering into the Promised Land: "do not harden your hearts as in the rebellion." Throughout Scripture we can see the things that lead to having a stubborn heart. The first thing is to be self-centered as were the children of Israel during the time of the

Judges. We are told that during that season that "everyone did what was right in their own eyes." Sounds much like our modern society. When the cry of a people is "It is my right to do as I please" you will find a people that have stubborn hearts. They refuse to see what the will of God is because they are only focus upon themselves. When Christians begin to place their own agendas before the will of God you find Churches that are run by men's self-will and not God's will. Next you find individuals, though they are self-centered in their focuses, have a social conscience because they do what they do because "they think they will be seen of men." They desire the glory of men instead of pleasing God. These actions lead to spiritual contamination because those that live for themselves "do not like to retain God in *their* knowledge." (Romans 1:28). We see the sequential consequences that occur from these actions which are that "we see that they could not enter into the rest of God because of unbelief.

Beware, Brethren that you do not allow unbelief to sidetrack you from the Lordship of Christ and hinder you from entering into the rest of your Lord.

VII. v. 4:1-11: The GOSPEL of
The Lordship of Christ

A. v. 1: Promise of God
   1. Requirement of Faith
      Hebrews 11:6: "But without faith it is impossible to please God: for he that cometh to God must believe that He is, and that He is a rewarder of them that diligently seek Him."
   2. Rest of The Faithful
      Matthew 11:28-30: "Come unto me all ye that labor and are heavy laden, and I will give your rest.

      Take my yoke upon you, and learn of me; for I am meek and lowly in heart: and ye shall find rest unto your souls.

      For my yoke is easy, and my burden is light."
   3. Reception of The Future
      John 14:1-6: "Let not your heart be troubled: ye believe in God believe also in me.

      In my Father's house are many mansions: if it were not so, I would have told you. I go to prepare a place for you.

      And if I go and prepare a place for you, I will come again and receive you unto myself; that where I am there ye may be also.

      And whither I go ye know, and the way ye know.
      … Jesus said unto Him, I am the way, the truth, and the life; no man comes unto the Father, but by me."

B. v. 2: Preached Gospel
  1. Foundation of The Power
     Romans 1:16-17: "For I am not ashamed of the gospel of Christ; for it is the power of God unto salvatioin to every one that believes; to the Jew first, and also to the Greek.
     For therein is the righteousness of God revealed from faith to faith; as it is written, The just shall live by faith."

  2. Foolish Perception
     1 Corinthians 1:22-24: "For the Jews require a sign, and the Greeks seek after wisdom:
     But we preach Christ crucified, unto the Jews a stumbling-block, and unto the Greeks foolishness;
     But unto them which are called, both Jews and Greeks, Christ the power of God, and the wisdom of God."
  3. Faith Leads to Profit – v. 2b
     "… but the word preached did not profit them, not being mixed with faith in them that heard it."

C. v. 3ff: Profitable Gift
   2 Timothy 3:16-17: "All Scripture is given by inspiration of God and is profitable for …"
  1. Beliefs = "doctrine"
  2. Betterment = "reproof & correction"
  3. Building of a Life = "instruction is righteousness"
  *. v. 11: BE = "be diligent to enter that rest"
     v. 17: that the child of God will be complete, thoroughly furnished unto all good works."

VII. v. 4:1-11: The Gospel of
    The Lordship of Christ
  A. v. 1: Promise of God
      There are still promises of God and of Christ that have been made to His people that have yet to be fulfilled. "Since a promise remains of entering His rest, let us fear lest any of you seem to have come short of it." If one is to enter into the rest of God there are some points that must be understood.
    1. Requirement of Faith
        Hebrews 11:6 tells us that "without faith it is impossible to please God: for he that comes to God must believe that He is, and that he is a rewarder of them that diligently seek Him." To make Christ one's Lord an individual must believe in the existence of God. There cannot be any doubt as to whether or not God is. One of the interesting things about Scripture is that is never argues for the existence for God. The Bible assumes that everyone believes that God is. God's Word tells us that "a fool has said in their heart there is no God." Anyone that denies the existence of God is considered a "fool" by God Himself. The Scriptures acknowledge that people may believe in false gods but anyone denying that God exists is a simple idiot. Even so, this required faith goes beyond believing that God exists it must also believe that God will reward those that follow Him by faith. Timothy is encouraged to "not be weary in well doing: for in due season you shall reap, if you faint not. " (Galatians 6:9). The spiritual law of return is "what you sow, you shall reap. If you sow sparingly you will reap sparingly and if you sow bountifully you will reap bountifully." God is rewarder of them that diligently seek Him.

2. Rest of The Faithful

Jesus invited "Come unto me all ye that labor and are heavy laden, and I will give you rest. Take my yoke upon you, and learn of me; for I am meek and lowly in heart: and ye shall find rest unto your souls." (Matthew 11:28-30). Jesus' invitation is not as simple as many would like to believe. First of all Jesus invited those that are busy with "labor." This invitation to come and receive rest is offered to those that are busy about the work of the Kingdom of Christ. This is not an invitation for those that are lazy or for those that have chosen to set back and take it easy. Secondly, this invitation is offered to those that are bearing "heavy burdens." This indicates individuals that have taken upon themselves the job of burden bearing. These burdens may be the needs of the Church, of others, and maybe some personal burdens that must be carried. This invitation is for those that have committed to carry those burdens and not to lay them aside and mourn them. In giving these "labors" and "burdens" to Jesus we are given to understand that we will take upon ourselves "Jesus' yoke" (His Lordship) and be willing to "learn from Jesus." This is not an invitation to set on the sidelines and watch others do the work. This invitation is to get involved in the "Kingdom work of Christ" and to be willing to learn what Jesus has to teach us in every situation of life. By doing so we are promised that we will find "rest for our souls."

3. Reception of The Future

Jesus commanded us: "Let not your heart be troubled: ye believe in God believe also in me.

In my Father's house are many mansions: if it were not so, I would have told you. I go to prepare a place for you.

And if I go and prepare a place for you, I will come again and receive you unto myself; that where I am there ye may be also.

And whither I go ye know, and the way ye know.

... Jesus said unto him, I Am The Way, The Truth, and The Life; no man comes unto the Father, but by me." (John 14:1-6).

Jesus has made it as simple as possible: He has promised to come back and take us home to be with Him forever. In 1 Thessalonians 4:13-18 we are informed concerning Jesus' return for us as His Church: verses 16 – 17 concentrate on this promise:

"For the Lord Himself will descend from heaven with a shout, with the voice of an archangel, and with the trumpet of God. And the dead in Christ will rise first. Then we who are alive and remain shall be caught up together with them in the clouds to meet the Lord in the air. **And thus we shall always be with the Lord**."

What a great promise to look forward to. This is the HOPE that we can hold on to while we live and wait for the fulfillment of Christ's promises.

B. v. 2: Preached Gospel

The first question that should be asked is: "What is the Gospel?" The Scriptural answer to that question is found in 1 Corinthians 15:1-11 (selected)

"Moreover, brethren, I declare to you the gospel which I preached to you, which also you received and in which you stand,

by which also you are saved, if you hold fast the word which I preached to you—unless you believed in vain.

For I delivered to you first of all that which I also received: that Christ died for our sins according to the Scriptures,

and that He was buried, and that He rose again the third day according to the Scriptures,

and that He was seen ...

Therefore, whether it was I or they, so we preach and so you believed."

Here we have the summation of the Gospel of Christ. This Gospel Message is the ...

1. Foundation of Power

    "For I am not ashamed of the gospel of Christ; for it is the power of God unto salvation to everyone that believes; to the Jew first, and also to the Greek.

    For there in is the righteousness of God revealed from faith to faith; as it is written, The just shall live by faith." (Romans 1:16-17).

    The Gospel of Jesus Christ is the power of God unto salvation to everyone that believes. This is the Gospel of the Lordship of Christ. This is the only message that has the power to bring someone into a right relationship with God. Men may try other religions, work, good deeds, buying their way in, or whatever. When men present their best before a righteous, holy God "they are all as an unclean *thing*, and all our righteousnesses *are* as filthy rags." (Isaiah 64:6). Only by accepting Jesus in the free pardon of our sin can we then make Him our Lord.

2. Foolish Perception

    Many when presented with the Gospel of Jesus Christ will refuse to accept it. "For the Jews require a sign, and the Greeks seek after wisdom: But we preach Christ crucified, unto the Jews a stumbling-block, and unto the Greeks foolishness; But unto them which are called, both Jews and Greeks, Christ the power of God, and the wisdom of God." (1 Corinthians 1:22-24). Here we are to understand that everyone will not automatically accept the message of salvation offered through Jesus Christ. We must be willing to do what is necessary to share the Gospel message of Christ with those that we might call "hard-sales." Peter gave us the example of how to do this with individuals that we can associate with the Jews. A "Jewish" kind of person is one that already has a basic understanding about the Bible and some simple Biblical doctrines like sin, death, resurrection. For these individuals the cross of Christ is a stumbling block. For these they must be shown the necessity of having their personal sins forgiven and that acceptance of the blood of Christ will do what is required. This type of preaching is seen in Acts 2:14-47. Peter was preaching to a group of listeners that already had the basic understanding about the existence of God and the problem of sin and death. They needed to understand about the resurrection of Jesus Christ and what He did for their personal sin. A "Greekish" kind of person is one that has no basic understanding of the Bible. These individuals have not been taught about creation, sin, death and the need for forgiveness of one's personal sins. These individual have a basic evolutionary outlook on life. They are individuals that try to explain life by materialistic means. In Acts 17:16-34 Paul gives us they type of preaching that is necessary to share with a "Greekish" type person. In verse 18 certain Epicurean and Stoic philosophers (who had a basic evolutionary outlook on life) said of the Gospel that Paul was preaching: "What does this babbler want to say?" They were completely without understanding. Paul then gives us a model of sharing the Gospel with evolutionary based individuals: in verse 24 he began with teaching them about God as the creator of all things. Then in verse 26 he explained that all men are descendants of one man (one blood). He then begins to explain that every person has the need to be forgiven by God for our sins. Finally explaining that Jesus came into the world and because He was raised from the dead we would be judged by His righteousness and not by man's standards. When they hear of the resurrection of the dead some mocked, while others said: We will hear you again on this matter. However, some men joined him and believed. What made the change in these individual from thinking Paul was a babbler to being willing to listen to his message was the fact that Paul began with creation and taught up to the resurrection of Christ. This is the model we should follow today in sharing the Gospel with our world.

3. v. 2b: Faith Leads to Profit

   Of those that did not enter into the rest that God was offering them it is said: "the word preached did not profit them, not being mixed with faith in them that heard it." For the Gospel of Christ to be of any profit to an individual that one must accept it by faith. Let us remember that "Faith comes by hearing and hearing by the word of God." (Romans 10:17).

C. v. 3ff: Profitable Gift

   We are told that when we accept the Gospel message of Christ and accept God's Word we then accept that … (2 Timothy 3:16-17) "All Scripture is given by inspiration of God and is profitable for…"

1. Beliefs = "doctrine"

   What one believes about life and living will determine the consequences of that life lived. The Bible should be our source for all of our understanding concerning both this life lived here on earth and about the life to be lived in the future eternity.

2. Betterment = "reproof & correction"

   If one heeds the Scriptures they will do two things to better one's existence. The first thing the Bible will do is to inform us of what is wrong (reproof). Then the Bible will give us the information that we need to repair the problems that are in our lives (correction).

3. Building of a Life = "instruction in righteousness"

   As a Christian we can be ready to live a successful life by following the instructions given to us by God. By following the Scriptural teachings "the child of God will be complete, thoroughly furnished unto all good works." (v. 17).

*. v. 11: BE = "be diligent to enter that rest"

   God desires to "give us the desires of our hearts" (Psalm 37:4) but can only do so when we choose to "trust in the Lord and do good; dwell in the land, and feed on God faithfulness. Delight ourselves also in the

Lord, commit our way to the Lord, trust also in Him, and He shall bring it to pass." (Psalm 37:3-5).

VIII. v. 4:12-16: The HOLY BIBLE of
The Lordship of Christ

A. v. 12: Heavenly Piercing
Intro. Scripture
1. Spiritual
2. Physical
3. Mental

B. v. 13-14: Holy Patron
1. Responsibility
"… we must give account"
2. Representative
3. Required
"… let us hold fast our confession"

C. v. 15-16: High Priest
1. v. 15b: Shared Our Struggling Experiences
2. v. 15a: Sympathizes with Our Sincere Efforts
3. v. 16a: Seeks our Singular Encounters

*. v. 16b: Source of Spiritual Energy
a. Forgiveness = "mercy"
b. Favor = "grace"
c. Freedom = "help in time of need"

••

VIII. v. 4:12-16: The HOLY BIBLE of
The Lordship of Christ
A. v. 12: Heavenly Piercing
Intro. Scripture
    Here we are given a specific detailed description of the Bible. The first thing that must be understood is that this collection of books is "the Word of God." God as mankind's creator has chosen to speak to us and has done so through "the Holy Scriptures, which are able to

make one wise for salvation through faith which is in Christ Jesus. For all Scripture is given by inspiration of God" (2 Timothy 3:15-16). Next we are to understand that The Bible is "a living and powerful" thing. We are given to understand that Jesus Himself was and is "the living Word of God" (John 1:1). The Bible is "The Written Word of God." Just as Jesus was and is living The Bible is also living and powerful. The Words of Scripture are just as relevant today as they were at the times of their writing. This is so because the Bible affects people {"sharper than any two-edged sword, piercing …"} in the three areas of life that make up a person's being.

1. Spiritual – "piercing even to the division of soul and spirit"

The Spiritual aspect of a person's life is the most important, yet often the most neglected, part of a person's being. Jesus said: "For what is a man profited, if he shall gain the whole world, and lose his own soul? or what shall a man give in exchange for his soul?" (Matthew 16:26). The purpose of God's Word is to "convert the soul; the testimony of the Lord is sure, making wise the simple" (Psalm 19:7).

2. Physical – "piercing even to the division of joints and marrow,"

God desires to save more than just the soul. God also desires to save the body. Paul encourages Christians to "Mortify therefore your members which are upon the earth; fornication, uncleanness, inordinate affection, evil concupiscence, and covetousness, which is idolatry: For which things' sake the wrath of God cometh on the children of disobedience: In the which ye also walked some time, when ye lived in them. But now ye also put off all these; anger, wrath, malice, blasphemy, filthy communication out of your mouth. Lie not one to another, seeing that ye have put off the old man with his deeds; And have put on the new *man*, which is renewed in knowledge after the image of him that created him" (Colossians 3:5-10).

3. Mental

God also has designed that salvation involve the mind. Paul informs us that we are "not to be conformed to this world, but be transformed by the renewing of the mind, that we may prove what is that good and acceptable and perfect will of God" (Romans 12:2). We can do this by following the instruction in Philippians 4:8 which says: "Finally, brethren, whatever things are true, whatever things are noble, whatever things are just, whatever things are pure, whatever things are lovely, whatever things are of good report, if there is any virtue and if there is anything praise worthy – meditate on these things." When a Christian does this "the peace of God, which surpasses all understanding, will guard their heart and mind through Christ Jesus" (Philippians 4:7).

B. v. 13-14: Holy Patron

Because God has given mankind His Word He has certain expectation of us.

1. Responsibility

God sees all things and nothing is hidden from Him. With this understanding we must also recognize that everyone is required to "give account" to Him. "It is appointed for men to die once, but after this the judgment" (Hebrews 9:27). There will be two judgments: "The Judgment Seat of Christ" which is for those whom have accepted Jesus as Savior; and "The Great White Throne Judgment" which will be for those whom refused to accept God's forgiveness which is found in Jesus Christ.

2. Representative

There is one God, and one mediator between God and men, the man Christ Jesus" (1 Timothy 2:5). It is by "the name of Jesus Christ of Nazareth whom was crucified, whom God raised from the dead *that life is given.* ... Nor is there salvation in any other, for there

is no other name under heaven given among men by which we must be saved" (Acts 4:10-12).
3. Required
Once people have accepted God's salvation that is offered only in Jesus Christ those individuals are expected to "hold fast their confession." A Christian can profess a good confession by "giving all diligence, add to one's faith virtue, to virtue add knowledge, to knowledge add self-control, to self-control add perseverance, to perseverance add godliness, to godliness add brotherly kindness, and to brotherly kindness add love. For if these things are yours and abound, you will be neither barren nor unfruitful in the knowledge of our Lord Jesus Christ" (2 Peter 1:5-8).

C. v. 15-16: High Priest

Jesus has become our High Priest by entering into the Holy of Holies with His own blood and making intercession for us that our sin would be forgiven by the Father. He is our Great High Priest in that He ...

1. v. 15a: Sympathizes with Our Sincere Efforts
Jesus can empathize with us because He "became flesh and dwelt among us" (John 1:14). Jesus experienced all aspects of life so He can understand our plight.

2. v. 15b: Shared Our Struggling Experiences
Jesus "was in all points tempted as we are, yet without sin." Jesus understands the struggles that we experience when we are "tempted being drawn away by our own desires and enticed" (James 1:14).

3. v. 16a: Seeks our Singular Encounters
Because Jesus is our Great High Priest, and because of what He along has done for us, we can "therefore come boldly to the throne of grace." As we approach God through Jesus Christ we can obtain the ...

*. v. 16b: Source of Spiritual Energy
   a. Forgiveness = "mercy"

      The first thing that every individual needs from God is mercy. A simple definition of mercy is "not receiving what we deserve {ie. Hell}. "The wages of sin is death" {Hell} Romans 6:23. "For all have sinned and come short of the glory of God" (Romans 3:23). We find this forgiveness only in Jesus "for He came to save His people from their sins" (Matthew 1:21).

   b. Favor = "grace"

      Every individual also needs grace. A simple definition of grace is "receiving what one could never deserve {ie. a right relationship with God}. Christ has given mankind an opportunity to come into a right relationship with God the Father. "He who abides in the doctrine of Christ has both the Father and the Son" (2 John 9).

   c. Freedom = "help in time of need"

      "Therefore humble yourselves under the mighty hand of God, that He may exalt you in due time, casting all your care upon Him, for He cares for you. Be sober, be vigilant; because you adversary the devil walks about like a roaring lion, seeking whom he may devour. Resist him, steadfast in the faith knowing that the same sufferings are experienced by your brotherhood in the world. But may the God of all grace, who called us to His eternal glory by Christ Jesus, after you have suffered a while, mature, establish, strengthen, and settle you. To Him be the glory and the dominion forever and ever. Amen" (1 Peter 5:6-11).

     Only by accepting Jesus Christ as the living Word of God and accepting the Bible as the written Word of God can one make Jesus Christ their Lord.

IX. v. 5:1-11: The Inspiration of
The Lordship of Christ

A. v. 5:1-3: Problem with Man's Priesthood
  1. v. 1: Source of Authority is Tainted
     "For every high priest taken from among men is appointed for men in things pertaining to God, that he may offer both gifts and sacrifices for sins."
  2. v. 2: Seeker of The Almighty's Truth
     "He can have compassion on those who are ignorant and going astray, since he himself is also subject to weakness."
  3. v. 3: Sinner Among Transgressors
     "Because of this he is required as for the people, so also for himself, to offer sacrifices for sins."

B. v. 5:4-7: Pictured by The Messiah's Priesthood
  1. v. 4-5: Acknowledged Son
     "And no man takes this honor to himself, but he who is called by God, just as Aaron was.
     So also Christ did not glorify Himself to become High Priest, but it was He who said to Him:
        "You are My Son.
        Today I have begotten You.""
  2. v. 6: Acceptable Source
     "God so says in another place:
        "You are a priest forever
        according to the order of Melchizedek.""
  3. v. 7: Answered Supplications
     "who, in the days of His flesh, when He had offered up prayers and supplications, with vehement cries and tears to Him who was able to save Him from death, and was heard because of His godly fear;"

C. v. 5:8-11: Perfecting of The Master's Priesthood
      1. v. 8: Course of Learning = Suffering
            "though He was a Son, yet He learned obedience by the things which He suffered."
      2. v. 9: Completed Lordship = Sacrifice
            "and having been perfected, He became the author of eternal salvation to all who obey Him."
      3. v. 10: Consecrated Linage = Source
            "called by God as High Priest according to the order of Melchizedek."
      *. v. 11 Contemplation Longed-For = Sharing
            "of whom we have much to say, and hard to explain, since you have become dull of hearing."

■■

IX. v. 5:1-11: The Inspiration of
               The Lordship of Christ
   A. v. 5:1-3: Problem with Man's Priesthood
         We understand that the Old Testament priesthood was not a perfected priesthood for several reasons. This priesthood that was according to the order of Aaron had three main problems.
      1. v. 1: Source of Authority was Tainted
            Every priest that served under this model of the priesthood was "taken from among men and appointed by men." Their authority was given to them by men. This being so their authority was limited to "things <u>pertaining</u> to God, that he may offer both gifts and sacrifices for sins." He could only be a picture of the true and not the real thing.
      2. v. 2: Seekers of The Almighty's Truth
            The second problem was that not even one priest that served under this model of priesthood knew all of the Truth. They all were only men and only knew what had been revealed to them through Moses. Therefore they, as with all men, were "ignorant and going astray."
         They may have done their best, but their best was never enough.

3. v. 3: Sinners Among Transgressors
   The main problem with the priests serving under the Aaron model of priesthood was that they were sinners just like the ones that they represented. They had to offer sacrifices for their personal sin before they could offer sacrifices for the sins of the people. They could never bring complete forgiveness for the sins of the people.
B. v. 5:4-7: Pictured by The Messiah's Priesthood
   Jesus' priesthood is better and greater than the Aaron's model of priesthood and therefore He should be our Lord. The reasons His priesthood is greater are …
1. v. 4-5: Acknowledged Son of The Almighty
   When and individual was appointed to be a priest that individual was to be chosen and not a volunteer. This was seen in the Aaron model of priesthood. Jesus was chosen to be the Great High Priest by God Himself and God also chose to appoint His own Son to represent sinful man to Him. Jesus' priesthood is greater because He is the Son of God and is appointed by the Father.
2. v. 6: Acceptable Source of Authority
   The authority for Jesus' priesthood was not from man. He was appointed by God. Also His priesthood was not modeled after the priesthood of man but was based upon "the order of Melchizedek." This order of priesthood will be dealt with further in a future message. Here it must be said that Jesus' authority was heavenly and not earthly.

3. v. 7: Answered Supplications from Above

When Jesus prayed He knew of an assurance that the Father heard Him and would answer Him. Jesus said when He prayed: "Father, I thank You that You have heard Me. And I know that You always hear Me, but because of the people who are standing by I said this *publically*, that they may believe that You sent Me" (John 11:41-42). Because Jesus and the Father are one, when Jesus prays He always prays is the will of the Father and will be answered accordingly.

C. v. 5:8-11: Perfecting of The Master's Priesthood

Jesus' priesthood was always perfect before the Father. This perfection is seen by men in Jesus' …

1. v. 8: Course of Learning = Suffering

We are told that "though Jesus was a Son, yet He learned obedience by the things which He suffered." The Greek word here for learned is "Manthano" or "Manthano" which means "to bring into experience." The Geek word here for "obedience is "Hupakow" or "Hupakoe" which means "to have willing subjection to that which is in the sphere of divine revelation." Hence, Jesus experienced the willing subjection to that which the Father had revealed for Him to do which He could not have experienced until He took upon Himself "the form of a servant" {ie.- a human body}.

2. v. 9: Completed Lordship = Sacrifice

The Greek word for "perfected" is "Teleioo" or "Teleioo" which means "to be made complete by the reaching of one's prescribed goal." Jesus came for the purpose of dying on the cross of Calvary and to shed His blood for our sins. His lordship was completed as He died for the sins of men. Jesus is "the author of eternal salvation to all who obey Him."

3. v. 10: Consecrated Linage – Source

The authority that Jesus has to be the Great High Priest is His because He is "called by God as High Priest according to the order of Melchizedek" and not chosen by men after the order of Aaron.

*. v. 11: Contemplation Longed-For – Sharing

The author of Hebrews shares his desire to give much more information concerning this order of Melchizedek. Realizing that his readers are not ready for that information he informs them that this is an issue that "is hard to explain, since they had become dull of hearing." When the author of Hebrews deals with this issue later in our study there are still questions that are left unanswered. To many today this is still a hard issue to explain and to find answers to. Some questions may never be answered here and we will have to wait until we arrive in Heaven to receive those answers because then "we will know as we are known."

X. v. 5:12 – 6:8: The Journey to
The Lordship of Christ

A. v. 5:12-14: A Christian-Child's Upbringing
  1. v. 12: Potential Mentioned
     a. Neglected Spirituality
        "for though by this time you ought to be teachers"
     b. Needed Schooling
        "you need someone to teach you again the first principles of the oracles of God"
     c. Necessary Simplicity
        "and you have come to need milk and not solid food"
  2. v. 13: Partakers of Milk
     a. Insincerity {implied}
        "for everyone who partakes only of milk"
     b. Inability
        "is unskilled in the word of righteousness"
     c. Immaturity
        "for he is a babe"
  3. v. 14: Process of Maturity
     a. Divine Sustenance
        "but solid food belongs to those who are of full age"
        Jesus said: "I have food to eat of which you do not know" speaking of spiritual food.
     b. Developed Senses
        "those who by reason of use have their senses exercised"
     c. Discerning Spirit
        "to discern both good and evil"

B. v. 6:1a: A Christ-Centered Unction
   "Therefore, leaving the discussion of the elementary principles of Christ"
  1. Doctrine of Christ – 2 John 9
     "whoever transgresses and does not abide in the doctrine of Christ does not have God. He who abides in the doctrine of Christ has both the Father and the Son."

2. Discipline – "leaving (maturing in) the doctrine"
   Ephesians 4:15b: "may grow up into Him in all things, which is the head, even Christ."
3. Direction
   "let us go on unto perfection" = Christ-likeness

C. v. 1b-8: A Correct-Christian Understanding
  1. v. 1b-3: Right Passions
     a. v. 1b: Foundation of Salvation
        "not laying again the foundation of repentance from dead works and of faith toward God"
     b. v. 2: Faith of The Saved
        "of the doctrine of baptisms, of laying on of hands, of resurrection of the dead, and of eternal judgment."
     c. v. 3: Future of the Sanctified
        "and this we <u>will do</u> if God permits"
  2. v. 4-6: Rejected Presentation
     a. Wrong Sight – "enlightenment"
        "and have tasted of the heavenly gift"
            Grasp of The Truth   but
                No Essence of The Truth
     b. Wrong Schooling – "partakers of the Holy Spirit"
        John 3:10: to Nicodemus Jesus said: "Are you the teacher of Israel, and do not know these things?"
            Guide to The Truth   but
                Not Educated in The Truth
     c. Wrong Seeking – v. 5:
        "and have tasted the good word of God and the powers of the age to come"
            Gospel of The Truth   but
                Not an Ear for The Truth
        2 Timothy 4:3: "For the time will come when they will not endure sound doctrine, but according to their own desires, because they have itching ears, they will heap up for themselves teachers, having itching ears;"

*. v. 6: Wicked Refusal
      "if they fall away, to renew them again to repentance, since they crucify again for themselves the Son of God, and put Him to an open shame."
   3. v. 7-8: Recognized Performance
      a. Bearing = all get the rain from God
         "for the earth which drinks in the rain that often comes upon it"
      b. Blessed = bears useful herbs – blessed of God
         "and bears herbs useful for those by whom it is cultivated, receives blessing from God"
      c. Burned = bears thorns and briers – it is rejected
         "but if it bears thorns and briers, it is rejected and near to being cursed, whose end is to be burned."
   *. What Will You BELIEVE about the Gospel

●●●

X. v. 5:12 – 6:8: The Journey to
            The Lordship of Christ
   We must always remember that when an individual accepts Jesus Christ as their Savior they begin the spiritual journey as a "baby." The New Birth begins a "New Spiritual Life." Just as physical babies should grow spiritual babies should grow. Spiritually we are encouraged to "grow up in all things into Him who is the head—Christ" (Ephesians 4:15). The progression from Jesus just being our Savior to Him being our Lord is a spiritual journey of growth.
   A. v. 5:12-14: A Christian-Child's Upbringing
      1. v. 12: Potential Mentioned
         The readers of the book of Hebrews should have grown in Christ to the point where they could be teaching others. But apparently they had neglected the spirituality to the point that they still needed someone to teach them. They still needed spiritual "milk" instead of spiritual "solid food." "Milk refers to food that has been predigested by someone else to make it easier to ingest – or understand. "Solid food" refers to

the more complex doctrines of the Bible that take study to understand and to apply to life. These hearers had the potential to learn but had not used it to grow spiritually and therefore were still spiritual babies.
2. v. 13: Partakers of Milk

It should be stated that there is nothing inherently wrong with being a spiritual baby. Every Christian starts their spiritual life that way. There is a problem with someone whom remains a spiritual baby for a long period of time. This spiritual babies were those that "partook <u>only of milk</u>." The implication is that they did not desire to grow spiritually and wanted to remain "unskillful in the word of righteousness" having remained "babies."
3. v. 14: Process of Maturity

To grow spiritually one must desire not only "the milk of the word" but also want the "more solid food" of the word of God. As one begins to take in the more substantial Scriptures and learn of them they will begin to grow to a "full age" into Christ. By allowing the word of God to "exercise their senses by reason of use" an individual will learn to "discern both good and evil."

B. v. 6:1a: A Christ-Centered Unction

The encouragement here is to grow spiritually to the point where one does not have to continually repeat the basic teachings of the Gospel of Christ. Although the message of salvation in Christ is to be a center focus of the Christian's message the Christian himself is charged with further learning concerning the things of God. Concerning this we need to understand the …
1. Doctrine of Christ – 2 John 9

"Whoever transgresses and does not abide in the doctrine of Christ does not have God. He who abides in the doctrine of Christ has both the Father and the Son." God's Word makes it clear that a person cannot have a right relationship with the Father if the Son {Jesus Christ} is rejected. Jesus Himself said: "I am The Way, The Truth, and The Life. No man comes to the

Father but by Me" (John 14:6). There is no other way to be acceptable to God except through Christ Jesus. This means that anyone whom rejects Jesus rejects the Father. There is no other mediator between God and man except for Jesus Christ.
2. Discipline – "leaving (going on from) the doctrine"
The idea here is that each Christian should be "growing in the grace and knowledge of our Lord and Savior Jesus Christ" (2 Peter 3:18). One's life should show that Jesus is Lord by the attitudes and actions that prevail. Also one's personal knowledge concerning God, Jesus, the Bible, and all spiritual things should continue to increase.
3. Direction – "let us go on unto perfection"
Again, the word for "perfection" means "completion." 2 Timothy 3:16-17 gives us an understanding of what is meant here. "All Scripture is given by inspiration of God, and is profitable for doctrine, for reproof, for correction, for instruction in righteousness, that the child of God may be complete, thoroughly equipped for every good work." Our spiritual growth should lead us to knowing what we believe, how to act, to know good and evil, and to be equipped to do the work of God.

C. v. 1b-8: A Correct-Christian Understanding
Here Paul is encouraging Christians to "grow up into Christ in all things." Part of the journey toward the Lordship of Christ is growing in the grace and knowledge of Christ. This spiritual growth is a positive sign that one has made Christ their Lord.
1. v. 1b-3: Right Passions
As the Child of God grows and learns more about Christ and Christian doctrine their understanding should move from the simple beliefs ("the foundation of repentance from dead works and of faith toward God") to an understanding of deeper issues ("of the doctrine of baptisms, of laying on of hand, of resurrection of the dead, and of eternal judgment"). In doing so a

Christians become better able to share their faith with others.
2. v. 4-6: Rejected Presentation &
3. v. 7-8: Recognized Performance

Watch this carefully. See if I read it correctly. "For it is *quite* possible for those who were once enlightened, and have tasted the heavenly gift, and were made partakers of the Holy Ghost, and have tasted the good word of God, and the powers of the world to come, if they shall fall away, to renew them again unto repentance; seeing they crucify to themselves the Son of God afresh, and put Him to an open shame." Is that what it says? You believe that a man can be once enlightened, made a partaker of the Holy Ghost, can taste the good Word of God and the powers of the world to come, but fall away and then repent—don't you? That is what all the folk believe who do not believe in the eternal security of the believer. What are you going to do with the backslider? If backsliding and apostasy are the same, don't you see this passage is the worst possible passage in the entire Bible for their favorite doctrine?

If those who hold that a man can be saved over and over again will ponder this passage, I am sure they will see how fatally it knifes their theory.

This is the way it reads: "For it is impossible for those who were once enlightened, and have tasted of the heavenly gift, and were made partakers of the Holy Ghost, and have tasted of the good Word of God, and the powers of the world to come, if they shall fall away to renew them again unto repentance; seeing they crucify to themselves the Son of God afresh, and put Him to an open shame." If this passage teaches that a man once saved can be lost again, then it also teaches that if that man is lost again, he can never repent and be saved. In other words, if the passage teaches that a man once saved can be lost again, it teaches that if you have ever been saved and you are now lost, you have a one-way ticket for hell, and there is no turning back. But what is the real question here? It is almost impossible to explain it in a minute or two, for you need to study the entire fifth and sixth chapters of Hebrews together.

The apostle is speaking to people who have the Old Testament and have been intellectually convinced that Jesus is the Messiah but who are exposed to persecution if they confess His name. Even if not genuine, they know that Jesus is the Messiah, and they must have felt the power and seen the evidence of His authority in the miracles wrought. Yet they can turn their backs upon it all and go back to Judaism and go into the synagogue again and say, "We do not believe Jesus Christ is the Messiah, the Son of God; we refuse the authority of this man. He should be crucified." "They crucify to themselves the Son of God afresh, and put Him to an open shame." The apostle says, "Do not try to do anything there; you cannot, for they have gone too far. They are apostate." It proves that they are not real Christians. In verse 9 we read, "But, beloved, we are persuaded better things of you, and things that accompany salvation, though we thus speak." That is, you could have all these things and not have salvation. You say, "I don't think so." No one could listen to a gospel address without being enlightened. "The entrance of Thy words giveth light; it giveth understanding unto the simple" (Psalm 119:130).

"... and have tasted of the heavenly gift." It is one thing to taste; it is another thing to eat. Many a person has gone that far and never been saved. The angel said to Ezekiel, "Son of man, eat this roll." But the angel saw that Ezekiel had only tasted it, so he commanded, "Son of man cause thy belly to eat it." It was in his mouth, and if his head had been cut off all the truth would be gone, but "God desires truth in the inwards parts."

"...and were made partakers of the Holy Ghost." They were neither sealed, nor indwelt, nor baptized, nor filled with the Spirit. He does not use one of the terms that refer to the Spirit's great offices, but says, "and were made partakers of the Holy Ghost." Did you ever see a man in a meeting where the Spirit of God was working in power, and have you ever gone over and talked to him and said, "Don't you want to come to Christ?" And he has answered, "I know I ought to come, I can feel the power of the Spirit of God in this meeting. I know this thing is right and I ought to yield, but I don't want to, and I won't" And he goes away resisting the Spirit although he was a partaker. So these people described in Hebrews 6 had been in this way outwardly acquainted with Christianity, but they now denied it all. For such there could be no repentance.

Now in order to prove that this is the correct interpretation of the passage, let me draw your attention to Hebrews 6:7-9: "For the earth which drinketh in the rain that cometh oft upon it, and bringeth forth herbs meet for them by whom it is dressed, receiveth blessing from God: but that which beareth thorns and briers is rejected, and is nigh unto cursing; whose end is to be burned. But, beloved, we are persuaded better things of you; you have gone farther than these apostates ever did, you have been saved; and so do not think we are confounding you with people like these." He uses this little parable to make clear what he means. Here are two pieces of grass growing side by side, we will say, just separated by a fence. The earth is the same, the same sun shines on them both, the same kind of rainfall waters them both. When the time of harvest comes, one of these plots brings forth herbs, but the other only thorns and briers. What is he teaching here? This is a message to the Jews, trying to make them see the reality of Christ's Messiahship and His fulfillment of all the types of old. These two plots of ground are two men; they are the hearts of two men. We may think of them in this way to make it all more graphic. They grow up side by side; they both are taught the Bible; they both go to the same synagogue; both wait for the Messiah; both go down and listen to John the Baptist preach; perhaps both were baptized by John the Baptist, confessing their sins. John's baptism was not salvation; it was just looking forward to the coming of a Savior. Both of them hear the Lord Jesus; both of them see Him do His works of power; both are in the crowd watching when He dies; both are there when the throngs go out to see the open tomb; both are near when He ascends to heaven; both see the mighty work of the Spirit on the day of Pentecost; both of them move in and out among the apostles; and outwardly you could not see any difference between them. But by-and-by persecution breaks out. One of them is arrested, and they say to him, "Deny Jesus Christ or you will die." He says, "I cannot deny Him; He is my Savior." "Then you will die." The first one declares. "I am ready to die, but I cannot deny Him." The other one is arrested and they say, "You must deny Christ or die." He says, "I will deny Him rather than die. I will go back and be a good Jew again rather than die." "Come out here, then," they command him.

They had a terrible way of taking him back. I remember reading how in such a case, they took him to an unclean place where a man slew a sow, and this one going back to Judaism, in order to prove his denial, spits on the blood of the sow and says, "So count I the blood of Jesus the Nazarene." And then they purify him and take him back. Could any real believer in Jesus do that? What made the difference between the two?

Those plots of ground had the same rain, the same sunshine, but there were different crops. What was the difference? One of them had the good seed and brought forth good fruit; the other did not have the good seed and brought forth thorn and briers. These two men were both familiar with the truth, but one received the incorruptible seed, the Word of life, and brought forth unto God. The other never received the good seed, and the day comes when he is an apostate.

If you will keep in mind the difference between an apostate and a backslider, it will save you a lot of trouble over many Scriptures. The apostate knows all about Christianity but never has been a real Christian. The backslider is a person who has known Christ, who did love Him, but became cold in his soul. There is not a Christian who has not often been guilty of backsliding. That is why we need the Lord as our advocate to restore our souls. When backslidden, it is not our union with Him that is destroyed but it is our communion. You may say, "Why are you so sure that a real Christian does not apostatize?" Because God says so in His Word. 1 John 2:18: "Little children, it is the last time: and as ye have heard that antichrist shall come, even now are there many antichrists; whereby we know that it is the last time." Antichrist means "opposed to Christ." The apostate is always a man opposed to Christ. A man says: "I have tried it all, and there is nothing in it," and so denounces Christ. "They went out from us, but they were not of us; for if they had been of us they would no doubt have continued with us: but they went out, that they might be made manifest that they were not all of us." The words "no doubt" are in italics and really cast a doubt. Leave those words out for they do not belong in the Greek text, and read it, "They went out from us, but they were not of us: for if they had been of us, they would have continued with us." And then he adds, "They went out, that they might be made manifest that they were not altogether (that is the literal rendering) of us" (1 John 2:19). In other words, they were with us in profession, in outward fellowship, but not altogether of us, because they had never really been born of God.

*. What Will You Believe About The Gospel?

XI. v. 6:9-12: The Kindling of
The Lordship of Christ

Intro. Salvation's Accompaniment
    v. 9: "But, beloved, we are confident of better things concerning you, yes, <u>things that accompany salvation</u>, though we speak in this manner."
1. Source of Love
   a. Concern of God = Planning for the World
   b. Call of God = Prophecy to the World
   c. Conclusions Arranged by God =
       = He Presence in the World
2. Salvation's Legacy
   a. Cradle = Passion
   b. Cross = Price
   c. Carrying Away = Promise
3. Solution for The Lost
   a. Circumstances = Problems Generated by Sin
   b. Call of God = Plea Given to the Sinful
   c. Concern of God = Pardon Guaranteed by The Savior

A. v. 10: Seen Actions – Conscience of God
   1. Work of Love
   2. Labor of Love
   3. Ministry of Love

B. v. 11: Satisfying Assurance – Confidence of the Future
   1. Desire
   2. Diligence
   3. Determination

C. v. 12: Source of Alignment – Calling to Obey
   "imitate those who through faith and patience"
       *. Philippians 4:9: "The things which you learned and received and heard and saw in me, these do, and the God of peace will be with you."
   1. Spiritual Education – Learned
   2. Shared Encouragement – Received
   3. Spoken Exposition – Heard
   4. Seen Example – Seen in me

*. Salvation's Completion – "inherit the promises."
■■■

Intro. v. 9: Salvation's Accompaniment

The reason that the Christian faith makes us confident that better things will be in our lives is because of the "things that accompany salvation." Before we look at the things which accompany salvation and kindle the fires of excitement concerning the Christian life let us look at salvation itself:

1. Source of Love

Scripture gives us notice that the reason that we love God is because He first loved us. We see His love in the …

   a. Concern of God = Planning for the World

We are told that Jesus Christ was "slain before the foundations of the world were laid." God knew even before He created us that we would rebel and sin. Because of this foreknowledge He prepared a plan whereby mankind could be forgiven and come back into a right relationship with Him.

   b. Call of God = Prophecy to the World

Man, left to himself, would never seek God out. Therefore God has given mankind His Word {the Holy Bible} so that we might have the information that we need to come to Him. As we learned in Hebrews 1:1-2: "God, who at various times and in various ways spoke in time past to the fathers by the prophets, has in these last days spoken to us by His Son." Today we have the New Testament which is the witness given to us of Jesus Christ, God's Son. Not only do we have God's Word but we also are given the presence of the Holy Spirit that "convicts the world of sin, and of righteousness, and of judgment: of sin, because they do not believe in Jesus; of righteousness, because Jesus has returned to heaven to be with the Father; and of judgment, because the ruler of this world is judged" (John 16:9-11). Jesus has given a call for the lost to "Come unto Me, all you who labor and are heavy laden, and I will give you rest. Take My yoke upon you and learn from Me, for I am gentle and lowly in heart, and

you will find rest for your souls. For My yoke is easy and My burden is light" (Matthew 11:28-30).
- c. Conclusions Arranged by God = Presence in the world

    God has done everything that is possible to invite the world to come to Him. However, the world must understand that to have a right relationship with God an individual must accept God's terms and not try to come to God based upon one's own agenda. God has arranged the final outcome based upon the acceptance or rejection of His Son, Jesus Christ. "For God so loved the world that He gave His only begotten Son, that whoever believes in Him should not perish ut have everlasting life. For God did not send His son into the world to condemn the world, ut that the world through Him might be saved. He who believes in Him is not condemned; but he who does not believe is condemned already, because he has not believed in the name of the only begotten Son of God. And this is the condemnation, that the light has come into the world, and men loved darkness rather than light, because their deeds were evil. For everyone practicing evil hates the light and does not come to the light, lest his deeds should be exposed. But he who does the truth comes to the light, that his deeds may be clearly seen, that they have been done in God" (John 3:16-21).

2. Salvation's Legacy

    The story of salvation is seen in the ...
  - a. Cradle = Passion of God

    "*Jesus* became flesh and dwelt among us, and we beheld His glory, the glory as of the only begotten of the Father, full of grace and truth" (John 1:14). God was working out His plan to bring salvation to mankind.

b. Cross = Price God Paid
     "... the love of God has been poured out in our hearts by the Holy Spirit who was given to us. For when we were still without strength, in due time Christ died for the ungodly. For scarcely for a righteous man will one die; yet perhaps for a good man someone would even dare to die. But God demonstrates His own love toward us, in that while we were still sinners, Christ died for us" (Romans 5:5-8).
  c. Carrying Away = Promise of God toward us
     Jesus said: "Let not your heart be troubled; you believe in God, believe also in Me. In My Father's house are many mansions; if it were not so, I would have told you. I go to prepare a place for you. And if I go and prepare a place for you, I will come again and receive you to Myself; that where I am, there you may be also" (John 14:1-3).
3. Solution for The Lost
  a. Circumstances = Problems Generated by Sin
     All mankind stands doomed because "the wages of sin is death" (Romans 6:23) and "all have sinned and fall short of the glory of God" (Romans 3:23). Everyone needs a Savior.
  b. Call of God = Plea Given to the Sinful
     Jesus cries: "Behold, I stand at the door and knock. If anyone hears My voice and opens the door, I will come in to him and fellowship with him, and he with Me" (Revelation 3:20).
  c. Concern of God = Pardon Guaranteed by the Savior
     "Believe on the Lord Jesus Christ, and you will be saved" (Acts 16:31). For "if we confess our sins, He is faithful and just to forgive us our sins and to cleanse us from all unrighteousness" (1 John 1:9).

Now let us look at some of the things that accompany salvation:

A. v. 10: Seen Actions – Conscience of God

An individual that has come to faith in Christ Jesus becomes aware of God's presence in their life. We are told that God is just and He recognizes the things that we strive to do for Him. He acknowledges our ...

1. Efforts = "work of love"

    The "work of love" is the things that we do as we strive to please our heavenly Father. We are commanded in Scripture to be "God-Pleasers" and not "men-pleasers." When we focus our lives upon doing what our Lord has asked us to do we give a proper witness to the world. Jesus said: "if you love Me, keep my commandments." He also said: "by this shall the world know that you are My disciples, in that you keep my commandments."

2. Energies = "labor of love"

    The "labor of love" is the intentional exertions that we give in order to complete the tasks that we striving to complete. This refers to the giving of our time and talents for the work of the Kingdom of Christ. When Jesus answered the question concerning what the greatest commandment was he said that we are to "love God with all our ... strength ...". This is the "labor" that we give to our Savior and Lord Jesus Christ.

3. Empathy = "ministry *of love*"

    As Christians our efforts and energies are to be focus upon "ministering to the saints." We can do this because we have experienced the same forgiveness of sins and have been given a new life in Christ. We share with one another as the family of God. "We know that we have passed from death to life, because we love the brethren" (1 John 3:14).

B. v. 11: Satisfying Assurance – Confidence of the Future
1. Desire

After a person has accepted Jesus Christ as their personal Savior their desires should change and begin to have a different center of attention. Paul shared with the Christians at the church of Colossae that "if you have been raised with Christ, seek those things which are above where Christ is, sitting at the right hand of God. Set your mind on things above, not on things on the earth" (Colossians 3:1-2). The Christian should strive "not to be conformed to this world, but to be transformed by the renewing of the mind, that we may prove what is that good and acceptable and perfect will of God" (Romans 12:2).

2. Diligence

The Christian should strive to do everything in their power to achieve the goals that Christ has set for them. "To this end I also labor, striving according to His working which works in me mightily" (Colossians 1:29). To do this one must be willing to make the necessary sacrifices. "Every man that strives for the mastery is temperate in all things. Now they would do it to obtain a corruptible crown; but we an incorruptible crown" (1 Corinthians 9:25).

3. Determination

The Christians is to live in "the full assurance of hope until the end." Paul expressed his meaning of this at the end of his life when he said that: "I am now ready to be offered, and the time of my departure is at hand. <u>I have fought the good fight, I have finished the race, I have kept the faith.</u> Finally, there is laid up for me the crown of righteousness, which the Lord the righteous Judge, will give to me on that Day, and not to me only but also to all who have love His appearing" (2 Timothy 4:6-8). At the end of his life he had hope that he would stand before his Lord Jesus Christ and hear Jesus say: "well done, thou good and faithful servant;

enter into the rest of your Lord." Paul's determined hope was express in three ways:
      a. Fought a good fight – he did not give up
      b. Finished the race – he completed his tasks
      c. Faithful to the end – he remained steadfast

C. v. 12: Source of Alignment – Calling to Obey

As the fires of the Lordship of Christ begin to grow in one's heart that individual is encouraged to follow the example of those who "through faith and patience" have come before. Paul encouraged us in Philippians 4:9 that "the things which you learned and received and heard and saw in me, these do, and the God of peace will be with you." There are four areas in life that a growing Christian can "imitate" based upon the faithful service of others. These are:

1. Spiritual Education – "learned"

The child of God should be a constant student of the teachings of God as revealed in the Holy Bible as interpreted by Jesus Christ. God the Father said of Jesus: "This is My beloved Son. Hear Him!" (Luke 9:35). Jesus said of Himself: "Learn from Me" (Matthew 11:29). The Bible says of itself: "All Scripture is given by inspiration of God, and it profitable for doctrine …" (2 Timothy 3:16). We are also commanded to "Study to show yourself approved unto God …" (2 Timothy 2:15). We must never stop learning from God and His Word.

2. Shared Encouragement – "received"

The things that have been "received" speak of the standards and teachings that have been <u>accepted</u> as the righteous things of God. Christians do not receive the teachings of other religions as acceptable and right. The early church was instructed that "Now therefore, you are no longer strangers and foreigners, but fellow citizens with the saints and members of the household of God, having been built on the foundation of the apostles and prophets, Jesus Christ Himself being the chief cornerstone" (Ephesians 2:19-20). The new

Christians that had come into the Church family understood that all the different beliefs that they had held before hand were now not acceptable (they were no longer strangers and foreigners). The foundation of the Christian faith and for all our beliefs is Jesus Christ Himself. The teachings of the apostles and the prophets as understood in Christ gave the Church its standard of belief and practice. We must always test any new teaching or new practice with the foundation that has been laid in Christ and by Scripture to see if it is acceptable or not. We are warned "if the foundations are destroyed, what can the righteous do?" (Psalm 11:3). We must always be careful to remain true to the foundation of Jesus Christ.

3. Spoken Exposition – "heard"

   "For the preaching of the cross is to them that perish foolishness; but unto us which are saved it is the power of God. for it is written, I will destroy the wisdom of the wise, and will bring to nothing the understanding of the prudent. Where is the wise? where is the scribe? where is the disputer of this world? Has not God made foolish the wisdom of this world? For after that in the wisdom of God the world by wisdom know not God, it pleased god by the foolishness of preaching to save them that believe" (1 Corinthians 1:18-21). We are commanded to "despise not prophesying" (1 Thess. 5:20). When God's Word is preached then it is to be heeded.

4. Seen example – "seen in me"

   God has provided the examples for us to follow if we are to live a life pleasing to Him. First, we are given the example of Christ Himself. Jesus came to show us how we should live in the Father's will. Next, we "are compassed about with so great a cloud of witnesses" (Hebrews 12:1) of those that have gone before us. We also have many great witnesses that are alive now and those that we live among.

*. Salvation's Completion – "inherit the promises"
    After all the things that we have experienced – "learned, received, heard, and seen in others – let us commit to follow their good examples of how to live for our Lord Jesus Christ. We will then be those who "through faith and patience inherit the promises."

XII. v. 6:13-20: The Lively Hope of
The Lordship of Christ

³ Blessed *be* the God and Father of our Lord Jesus Christ, which according to his abundant mercy hath begotten us again unto a lively hope by the resurrection of Jesus Christ from the dead,
⁴ To an inheritance incorruptible, and undefiled, and that fades not away, reserved in heaven for you,
⁵ Who are kept by the power of God through faith unto salvation ready to be revealed in the last time. (1 Peter 1:3-5).

A. v. 13-16: Representation of Hope
 1. Promoter of the Promise - God
 2. Personalized Promise – Name Changed
   a. Abram = father of many
   b. Abraham = father of many nations
 3. Performed Promise
   * - Birth of Isaac

B. v. 17-18: Respect of Hope
 1. Source of Comfort – Immutability of God"
 2. Strong Consolation – "God cannot lie"
 3. Satisfying Clutch – "lay hold of the hope set before us"

C. v. 19-20: Response to Hope
 1. Protection – "anchor of the soul"
   * - Willing Witness – Acts 1:8
     "But you shall receive power when the Holy Spirit has come upon you; and you shall be witnesses to Me in Jerusalem, and in all Judea and Samaria, and to the end of the earth."

    2. Presence of God – "behind the veil"
       * - Wonderful Worship – Micah 4:1-2
        "Now it shall come to pass in the latter days that the mountain of the Lord's house shall be established on the top of the mountains, and shall be exalted above the hills; and peoples shall flow to it."
        Many nations shall come and say, Come and let us go up to the mountain of the Lord;
        To the house of the God of Jacob;
        He will teach us His ways,
        And we shall walk in His paths.
        For out of Zion the law shall go forth,
        And the word of the Lord from Jerusalem."
    (1). Prophecy – in the latter days
    (2). Place of Worship – "the Lord's house established"
    (3). Plea – "come let us go up to the house of the Lord"
    (4). Ponder God's Word – "He will teach us His ways"
    (5). Path to Follow = "walk in His paths"
    (6). Pattern Set Forth = Law goes forth
    (7). Preaching of the Word of the Lord
    3. Priest "forever according to the order of Melchizedek"
       * - Walk Worthy – Ephesians 4:1
        "I, therefore, the prisoner of the Lord, beseech you to walk worthy of the calling with which you were called"

XII. v. 6:13-20: The Lively Hope of
                  The Lordship of Christ

    In 1 Peter 1:3-5 we are informed that this "lively hope" is given to us "by the resurrection of Jesus Christ from the dead." This hope that we have is determined to be promised, not based upon our ability, but is "kept by the power of God through faith unto salvation." This hope has already been "reserved in heaven for us" and will "be revealed in the last time." Hence, let us look at this hope.

A. v. 13-16: Representation of Hope
God is the promoter of this promised hope. "Because God could swear by no one greater, He swore by Himself, saying to Abraham: 'Surely blessing I will bless you, and multiplying I will multiply you.'" Abraham made this promised hope personal. Remember His name was "Abram" which meant "father of many." After God gave him this promised hope he changed his name to "Abraham" which means "father of many nations." Remember also that he changed his name at a time when he did not have any children at all. He had faith, and this faith was counted unto him as righteousness. This hope was represented when Isaac was born giving a physical aspect of a performed promise.

B. v. 17-18: Respect of Hope
Just as Abraham had respect toward the hope that God has given him in this promise of a future was also can have hope in the promises that God has given to us. We can have respect toward our hope in God because God is the source of our comfort. These verses speak of the "immutability of God." God is completely trust-worthy. Being confident of this very thing, that He which hath begun a good work in you will perform *it* until the day of Jesus Christ" (Philippians 1:6). Because God is completely trust-worthy we can have strong consolation in the fact that "God cannot lie." What He has said He will do. Based upon these two things we can have a satisfying clutch on this hope because we can "lay hold of the hope set before us" and make it ours personally.

C. v. 19-20: Response to Hope
Based upon the hope that we have in God through faith in our Lord Jesus Christ our lives should be changed and correspond to what God has done in us through salvation. We see this change in …

1. Protection – "anchor of the soul"

    This hope acts as an "anchor of the soul." It secures us in the work of Christ. We understand that Jesus is "the author and finisher of our faith" (Hebrews 12:2). We become so secure in Christ that we become <u>Willing Witnesses</u>. Jesus gave us as His disciples the promise that we have "received power when the Holy Spirit came upon us; and we will be witnesses to Him in Jerusalem, and in all Judea and Samaria, and to the end of the earth" (Acts 1:8).

2. Presence of God – "behind the veil"

    Being "behind the veil" refers to the "veil" in the Tabernacle that separated the Holy Place from the Holy of Holies. During the Old Testament days individuals did not have personal access to the presence of God. Only the high priest (and only one time a year) had the privilege to enter into the Holy of Holies and be in the presence of God. At the death of Christ the entrance into God's presence was given to every believer {as represented by the tearing of the veil in the Temple from top to bottom – Matthew 27:50-51}. The Old Testament prophet Micah referred to this in Micah 4:1-2 when he penned:

    > "Now it shall come to pass in the latter days that the mountain of the Lord's house shall be established on the top of the mountains, and shall be exalted above the hills; and people shall flow to it.
    >
    > Many nations shall come and say, Come and let us go up to the mountain of the Lord;
    > to the house of the god of Jacob; He will teach us His ways, and we shall walk in His paths. For out of Zion the law shall go forth, and the word of the Lord from Jerusalem."

    I believe here we find a reference to what would, and did, happen when Christ came. Here we see:

    (1). Prophecy – "in the latter days"
    (2). Place of Worship – "the Lord's House established"

  (3). Plea – "come let us go up to the house of the Lord"
  (4). Ponder God's Word – "He will teach us His ways"
  (5). Path to Follow – "walk in His paths"
  (6). Pattern Set Forth = "Law goes forth"
  (7). Preaching of the Word of the Lord
3. Priest "forever according to the Order of Melchizedek"

 We are given the ability to live the Christian life because we have a "High Priest" – the Lord Jesus Christ. "Therefore, we are encouraged to walk worthy of the calling with which we have been called" (Ephesians 4:1). We are to follow Christ's example and be lead by the internal presence of the Holy Spirit.

**XIII. v. 7:1-10: The Money Involvement of
            The Lordship of Christ**
A. v. 1-4: Order of Melchizedek
   1. v. : Earthly Positions
   2. v. 3: Eternal Priesthood
   3. v. 4: Education Prompted
 B. v. 5-7: Offering of Money
   1. v. 5: Tithe from the People
   2. v. 6: Testimony to the Promise
   3. v. 7: Test of the Pure
 C. v. 8-10: Operating Method
   1. v. 8a: Earthly Device
   2. v. 8b: Eternal Dividends
   3. v. 9-10a: Example Developed
   *. v. 10b: Effort of The Divine
       "Melchizedek met him"

****

XIII. v. 7:1-10: The Money Involvement of
            The Lordship of Christ
    It has truly been said: "That anything that one believes in will have the financial support of that one." Many feel that we should not speak about money: however, the Scriptures are full of information concerning the attitude towards, the belonging of, the concern about, the design for, the evil of, the focus upon, the gifting of, the how to of, the investment of, the juggling of, the kinds of, the love of, the misuse of, the need of, the ownership of, the power of, the qualities of, the righteous use of, the trouble cause by, the usury of, the value of, the wish for, the x-ploitation of, the yearning for, and the zeal caused by money. Therefore let us look at the "money involvement of The Lordship of Christ."

A. v 1-4: Order of Melchizedek

Although much is still not know concerning the individual Melchizedek, we here are given an example of the importance of the giving of the tithe. Melchizedek held an earthly position of which Abraham had respect for. Melchizedek is called the "king of Salem, king of righteousness, and the priest of the Most High God." He is further identified with the facts that he was "without father, without mother, without genealogy, having neither beginning of days, nor end of life, but made like the Son of God, remaining a priest continually." There are two prevailing views as to the identity of Melchizedek: the first is that he is an eternal being created to facilitate the worship of God both in the heavens and on earth. Those holding this view consider the characteristics mentioned to be literally understood. The Second view is that Melchizedek was actually Noah's son Shem. After the flood he became the first king of Salem {Jerusalem}. He was also the "priest of the Most High God" being the only remaining individual left surviving the flood. The characteristics concerning him being "without father, without mother, without genealogy, having neither beginning of days, nor end of life" simply refer to the fact that the order of priesthood that he had was one of a kind; not like anything before, nor would there ever be any kind like it to follow. Whichever was the case it is obvious that Abraham recognized his authority and was willing to "give a tenth of the spoils" to him.

B. v. 5-7: Offering of Money

We are now instructed as to how the offering of the People of God was taken. "The sons of Levi, who received the priesthood, were commanded to receive the tithes from the people according to the law." The Hebrews were to render a certain proportion (one-tenth) of the produce of the earth, trees, herds, etc., to the service of God (Lev. 27:30). This one-tenth went to the Levites, who had no part in the soil and were dependent upon their brethren for means of subsistence. The

Levites, in turn, gave one-tenth of what they received to the priests (Num. 18:26-28). Every third year, a special provision was made for the poor, either out of the regular tithe or in addition to it (Deut. 14:28-29). The earthly priesthood was thus given to the tribe of Levi. Melchizedek, it is pointed out was not from that tribe, "received tithes from Abraham and blessed him who had the promises." He was the one in covenant with God, to whom God had given exceedingly great and precious promises. These promises are both of the life that now is and of that which is to come; this honor have all those who receive the Lord Jesus, in whom all the promises are. Melchizedek's greater honor – in that it was his place and privilege to bless Abraham; and it is an uncontested maxim "that the lesser is blessed of the greater" (v. 7). He who gives the blessing is greater than he who receive it; and therefore he being a type of Christ, the Meritor and Mediator of all the blessings to all those who have accepted the free pardon of sin that God has offered in Jesus Christ, must be greater than all the priests of the order of Aaron.

C. v. 8-10: Operating Method

So how is this tithing to work? "Here mortal men receive tithes." This was and is God's method of supporting His Kingdom work here on earth. Many Christians today suggest that the "tithe" was strictly an Old Testament doctrine. This in point of fact may be the case; but even so, let us look at what the New Testament Scriptures actually says about giving.

Jesus condemned the scribes and Pharisees, calling them hypocrites, for having omitted "the weightier matters of the law (judgment, mercy, and faith) and in their place doing other deeds. Jesus pointed out that they did "tithe of mint and anise and cumin." Jesus then told them that they should be doing the weightier matters of the law and "not leave the other undone." So although Jesus did not strictly command the tithe He did commend the tithe.

Paul states the "Spiritual Laws Of Giving" in 2 Corinthians 9:6-15 which are:
1. v. 6: Governed Harvest

> The principle is simple: "You Reap What You Sow." One whom is stingy with the blessings that God has given them should expect nothing from God in continued blessings. A greedy heart stops the flow of blessings.

2. v. 7-8: Gift of The Heart
   a. Enthusiasm

   > It is true that the New Testament idea of giving is based upon "as one purposes in his heart." God does not desire that one give with a resentful heart nor does God desire one to give simply out of a sense of obligation. God would have us give out of a willing heart because of our appreciation for what He has done for us; spiritually, mentally, and physically.

   b. Exuberance

   > "God loves a cheerful giver." Giving out of a willing heart allows an individual to can give with a cheerful attitude. It has been said: "We should give until it hurts." I disagree: I believe that we should give until it starts feeling good.

   c. Expectation – Trust (v. 8)

   > Christians should base their giving upon their trust in God. We have been given the promise that "God shall supply all our need according to His riches in glory by Christ Jesus" (Philippians 4:19). The amount of our giving is directly related to the faith we have in God.

3. v. 9-12: Growth of the Helpful

Verse 9 gives us an outline of how giving is the result of the blessings of God upon the life of a man whom "fears the Lord". It is a quote from Psalm 112:9. This chapter is speaking about the "man who fears the Lord, who delights greatly in His commandments" (Ps. 112:1). After describing this man, the chapter continues with a list of blessings that individual will receive. This quote in 2 Corinthians is 3 of the last 4 blessings mentioned. We see the meaning of the quoted blesses expounded in the following three verses.

a. v. 10: Necessary Seed

"He has dispersed abroad." As God has supplied the proper necessities to share the one who sows (the Christian) shares the gifts with others. God has promised that if the gifts are shared that He will "multiply the seed that has been sown and increase the fruits of righteousness" in the giver's life.

b. v. 11: Need Seen

"He has given to the poor." "God will enrich in everything" the Christian who has caused there to be "thanksgiving to God" because of his giving to the poor. Understand that this "enrichment" is not necessarily "monetary" in nature as many today would have you believe. God's enrichment of our lives is reflected in the church in Smyrna when Jesus said of them that He "knew their works, tribulation, and poverty (<u>but you are rich</u>) …" (Revelation 2:9).

- c. v. 12: Nourished Saints

    "His righteousness endures forever." This individual reflects the righteousness of God through the "administration of this service that not only supplies the needs of the saints, but also is abounding in thanksgiving to God by many" because of the sharing of the gifts.

4. v. 13: Gospel of Honor

    There is a three-fold goal behind this ministry as proof of God working through us as His people. The three goals are to ...

    a. Glorify God the Creator

        To bring glory to God one must always begin with the beginning: "In the beginning God created the heavens and the earth" (Genesis 1:1). We as God's people continue to glorify God when we do "the Kingdom Work of Christ – "this ministry".

    b. Gospel of Christ Confessed

        The proof that our confession to Christ is real is seen in our "obedience of our confession to the gospel of Christ." If we are not obedient to Christ's will then our confession is false.

    c. Giving through the Church to Others

        This giving is to be made for a "liberal sharing with the church and with all men." I say that this giving is to be made "through the Church" because we are commanded "concerning the collection for the saints" to "on the first day of the week" ... "to lay something aside, storing up as He may prosper," (1 Corinthians 16:1-2). The church was to distribute those gifts as the Lord blessed them to do so.

5. v. 14-15: Grace of His Indescribable Gift
   When we have been blessed and are able to share with those in need we can then give …
   a. Prayers to God
      We will be able to "in everything give thanks: for this is the will of God in Christ Jesus for you" (1 Thessalonians 5:18).
   b. Passion of Grace
      We will begin to understand that we are "His." In this giving spirit you will learn that when "you were raised with Christ, you seek those things which are above, where Christ is, sitting at the right hand of God. You will Set your mind on things above, and not on things on the earth" (Colossians 3:1-2).
   c. Present of the Gift
      We will also begin to understand that Jesus Christ is "God's indescribable gift." When we accept Jesus Christ as our Savior and Lord we receive all that we need for this life and for the life to come.

In Closing, concerning the subject of "The Tithe" let me say:
  Abraham Commenced It
    Jacob Continued It
      Moses Commanded It
        Malachi Confirmed It
          Jesus Commended It
            Who are we to Cancel It!

XIV. v. 7:11-28: The New Order of The Lordship of Christ

A. v. 11-19: Giving of a New Priesthood
  1. v. 11-12: Necessity of Change
     a. v. 11a: Cessation of the Levitical Priesthood
     b. v. 11b: Consideration of The Lord's Priest
     c. v. 12: Change of the Law Precipitated
  2. v. 13-17: Need for Christ
     a. v. 13-14: Problem of the Law's Effort
     b. v. 15-16a: Priesthood of the Lord Evident
     c. v. 16-17: Power of Life Eternal
  3. v. 18-19: New Consideration
     a. v. 18a: Former
     b. v. 18b-19a: Failure
     c. v. 19b: Future
B. v. 20-24: Greatness of The New Priest
  1. v. 20-21: Sworn Oath
     a. Eternal Promise – "Jesus made a priest by and oath"
     b. Earthly Priest – "made without an oath"
     c. Edict Presented – God has spoken: v. 21
  2. v. 22: Sure Offer
     a. Great – "by so much more"
     b. Guarantee – "Jesus become surety"
     c. Greatest – "of a better covenant"
  3. v. 23-24: Steadfast Opportunity
     a. Priestly Process – "also there were many priests"
     b. Preventative Problem – "prevented by death"
     c. Permanent Solution – "Jesus continues forever, has an unchangeable priesthood"
C. v. 25-28: Gift of a New Perspective
  1. v. 25: Uttermost Salvation
  2. v. 26: Undefiled Separation
  3. v. 27: Ultimate Sacrifice
  *. v. 28: Unifying Son

****

XIV. v. 7:11-28: The New Order of
The Lordship of Christ

We now come to one of the central core issues found in this book dedicated to the Lordship of Christ. The Hebrews had lived all their lives based upon the Old Testament Sacrificial System. That system had now been completed in Jesus Christ and many of the Hebrews were having trouble making the change to the new order that was established. Let us consider now the need for a new priesthood, the greatness of the new priesthood, and the new understanding of how God would now work with His people.

  A. v. 11-19: Giving of a New Priesthood

    1. v. 11-12: Necessity of Change

God had given the Old Testament Sacrificial System to the Children of Israel as a pattern that could be followed to teach them of the saving work of salvation that would be completed in the coming Messiah {Jesus Christ}. The priesthood based upon the "order of Aaron" could not bring perfection to the people shown by the fact that the High Priest had to enter into the Holies of Holies once every year to offer a sacrifice for the people's sin. The sacrifice was a perpetual offering because it could never really forgive the sins of the people being only a symbol of the true. The coming Messiah {Jesus Christ} would be a priest not of the "order of Aaron, but "according to the order of Melchizedek." The result of the priesthood being changed is "of necessity also a change of the law."

    2. v. 13-17: Need for Christ

The new priesthood was based "not according to the law of a fleshly commandment, but according to the power of an endless life." All former High Priests' priesthoods came to an end because they all died. The new priesthood was based upon a Messiah that rose from the dead to live forever. This allows His priesthood to continue forever, for He never dies. Jesus became our High Priest by the oath of the Father and not by the law.

3. v. 18-19: New Consideration
The Old Testament System of Laws and Sacrifices was "annulled" being replaced with a "better" Opportunity that allows individuals to "draw near to God." The old system was "weak" because it was based upon the actions of men. If men failed to fulfill their duties then judgment would be certain to come. The old system was "unprofitable" because it enslaved men to a system of laws of which no one was capable of keeping. The old system also failed because it could "make nothing perfect." The Old Testament System could never bring mankind into a close personal relationship with God as our Father. "On the other hand" the new priesthood according to the order of Melchizedek brought "a better hope, through which we draw near to God."

B. v. 20-24: Greatness of The New Priest
Jesus' priesthood brings this "better hope" which gives mankind the opportunity to come into a right relationship with God the Father for three reasons:

1. v. 20-21: Sworn Oath
Jesus was made a priest, not by the law, but by "an oath." The Old Testament priest became priest because of their family linage. They were born into the right family and accepted the duties of the priesthood. Jesus was made a priest by the appointment of God Himself.

2. v. 22: Sure Offer
"Jesus has become a surety of a better covenant." Jesus came into the world, lived, died, arose the third day, and is now on the right hand of the Father making intercession for us as a guarantee of the promises of eternity that has been given to His disciples.

3. v. 23-24: Steadfast Opportunity
The priesthood of Christ is unchanging because "He continues forever" (He does not die). The Old Testament priest failed "because they were prevented, by death, from continuing."

C. v. 25-28: Gift of a New Perspective
  1. v. 25: Uttermost Salvation
    Jesus, based upon His eternal priesthood, can save completely those who come to God through Him. It must be understood that there is salvation only in Jesus Christ because He is the only one who "always lives to make intercession for people."
  2. v. 26: Undefiled Separation
    Part of the problem with the Old Testament priesthood is that those priests were just like every other person in that they were also sinners. They needed their sins forgiven them before they could serve in the office of priest and then they had to continually offer sacrifices for their personal sin to continue to serve in the office of priest. Jesus is "a High Priest whom is fitted for the office because He is holy, harmless, undefiled, and separate from sinners." He therefore has been exalted "higher than the heavens."
  3. v. 27: Ultimate Sacrifice
    In the Old Testament System the "high priest daily had to offer up sacrifices, first for his own sins and then for the people's." The high priest also had to go into the Holies of Holies once a year, every year, to offer up sacrifices for his own sin and for the sins of the people. Jesus offered the perfect sacrifice "when He offered up Himself, once for all."
  *. v. 28: Unifying Son
    The Old Testament priest were appointed by the Law of Moses but Jesus superseded the Law and by completing it on the Cross of Calvary. Now He has been appointed to be our High Priest by God the Father by an oath. Jesus' priesthood is greater because it lasts forever.

**XV. v. 8:1-13: The Operation of the New Order of
     The Lordship of Christ**
  A. v. 1-3 & 6: Main Point
    1. v. 1: Met The Binding Claims of God
       a. Savior – "we have a High Priest"
       b. Seated – Indicating a job that was complete
       c. Sovereign – "at the right hand of the throne of
                      the Majesty in the heavens"
    2. v. 2-3: Minister of The Believer's Connection
       a. Optimum Service – "a Minister of the sanctuary"
       b. Offer of Sacrifices – "offer both gifts and sacrifices"
       c. One Saving Gift – His own blood
    3. v. 6: Mediator of The Better Covenant
       a. Better Process – "more excellent ministry"
       b. Better Pledge – "better covenant"
       c. Better Promises
  B. v. 4-5: Model Pictured
    1. Legalistic – "law"
       * - Revealed our Sin
    2. Learned – "divinely instructed"
       * - Required Standard
    3. Lithographic – "copy and shadow"
       * - Replica of the Savior

  C. v. 7-13: Mode Perfected
    1. v. 7-9: Problematic Barrier – the old covenant of the law
       a. Distant – "made with their fathers"
       b. Disobeyed – "not continued in"
       c. Disregarded – as a people
    2. v. 10: Placement of Belief – Individual
    3. v. 11: Priesthood of the Believer - Involvement
    *. v. 12-13: Promised Benefit – Inclusion in God's Mercy

****

XV. v. 8:1-13: The Operation of the New Order of
     The Lordship of Christ
        Now we have this "New Order" of Priesthood we
   can ask: How does it differ from the old priesthood?

A. v. 1-3 & 6: Main Point
  1. v. 1: Met The Binding Claims of God
    God is holy, and therefore has certain claims required of His creation {mankind}. The first claim is that man requires a Savior or High Priest. Man's sinfulness prevents man from coming face to face with God. Jesus has come as "such a High Priest." The fact that He is now "seated" indicates that the job required of Him has been completed forever and that He will not have to redo the sacrifice again as earthly high priests had to. The fact the Jesus is "seated at the right hand of the throne of the Majesty in the heavens" indicates that He has satisfied the claims of God in regards to the forgiveness of the sins of men.
  2. v. 2-3: Minister of The Believer's Connection
    Jesus offered the optimum service for mankind in that His service was offered in the "sanctuary of the true tabernacle which the Lord erected and not man." Jesus made the "offer of both gifts and sacrifices" in the true Temple of God in Heaven and not on earth. The necessary offer that Christ had to give was that of His own blood which He shed at Calvary.
  3. v. 6: Mediator of The Better Covenant
    By this greater sacrifice and offering of His own blood Jesus "obtained a more excellent ministry" and became the "Mediator of a better covenant." This New Covenant {The New Testament} is better than the Old Covenant {The Old Testament} because it is "established on better (everlasting) promises."
B. v. 4-5: Model Pictured
    One needs to understand that the Old Covenant {The Old Testament model} was designed to be a picture of the true model of salvation that would be completed in Christ. The Old Testament Model gave us three things:

1. Legalistic – "law"
    * - Revealed our Sin
      The purpose of the law was to reveal to us our sins. By the law we understand what is wrong and what is right according to God and not according to the world's standards. The Old Testament Law acts as a mirror for one to gaze into and see their personal sins. Mirrors are not designed to help one become clean only to reveal the necessity of being cleaned.
2. Learned – "divinely instructed"
    * - Required Standard
      God gave Moses specific and stringent instructions concerning the building of the Tabernacle. God also gave orderly instructions concerning the model of worship that was to be followed. The reason that God gave and expected these directions to be adhered to in such detail was because they were representative of what the Messiah {Jesus Christ} would accomplish with His death on the cross.
3. Lithographic – "copy and shadow"
    * - Replica of the Savior
      The Tabernacle and the worship model that the Children of Israel followed served as "the copy and shadow of the heavenly things." When one looks closely at the Tabernacle and the sacrificial system Christ is clearly prefigured in every detail.

C. v. 7-13: Mode Perfected

Since the Old Testament model of worship could not bring complete forgiveness of sin for mankind because it was overseen by men acting as high priest (who died) and could not continue Christ came to perfect a mode of worship which would forever take care of the problem of sin and a broken relationship with God.

1. v. 7-9: Problematic Barrier – the old covenant of the law

   The Old Testament worship model has three main problems that cause it to become ineffective. These three problems were …

a. Distant – "made with their fathers"
      The Old Testament law and pattern of worship had been given to the forefathers of the participants. Because they had not been present or even alive when the law was given they had not made them their own. They did not "personalize" the law thus they …
   b. Disobeyed – "not continued in"
      The people chose not to obey the law given by God and the result was disastrous. The people left God and followed after their own lusts and desires to the point that God has no chose but to …
   c. Disregarded Them as a people
      God could no longer deal with the nation of Israel as a people dedicated unto Him. Their refusal to follow Him as their God led them into worship of false gods and thus they lost the actual practice of worship and also lost its meaning. Through Jesus Christ God took care of these problems by making faith and worship something that individuals can accept as their own. He did this in the New Testament (the New Covenant) by refocusing worship and faith into a …
2. v. 10: Placement of Belief – Individual
   The Old Covenant had the problem that the Law had been given in the past and individuals could not make it their own belief. In the New Covenant in Jesus Christ God "put His laws in the minds of believers and would write them in their hearts and would be their God and make them His people." Faith and Worship could now become personal and real for every individual.
3. v. 11: Priesthood of the Believer – Involvement
   Each individual would now have the ability {because of the presence of the Holy Spirit} to "know God." Reliance upon a restricted priesthood would no longer be necessary because now Jesus Christ would act personally as our High Priest being the mediator between God and man.

*. v. 12-13: Promised Benefit – Inclusion in God's Mercy

The promised benefit of the new order is three-fold. We are promised that God will cleanse us from our sins and that those sins will be remembered no more. Secondly, we are promised that we will now operate under the new covenant. We will no longer have the burden of offering continual sacrifices for our sins because Jesus Christ has made the perfect sacrifice once for all. And thirdly, because the old covenant is "becoming obsolete and growing old is ready to vanish away" we no longer burdened with the keeping of the Old Testament Law because Christ "wiped out the handwriting of requirements that was against us, which was contrary to us. And He has taken it out of the way, having nailed it to the cross. Having disarmed principalities and powers, He made a public spectacle of them, triumphing over them in it. So let no one judge you in food or in drink, or regarding a festival or a new moon or Sabbaths, which are a shadow of things to come, but the substance is of Christ" (Colossians 2:14-17 - NKJV).

XVI. v. 9:1-15: The Purification in
The Lordship of Christ
- A. v. 1-5: Presentation of The Sanctuary
  1. v. 1: Earthly Service
  2. v. 2: Entrance to the Sanctuary
     a. Lampstand   - **Potential**
     b. The Altar of Incense - **Power through Prayer**
     c. The Showbread   - **Privilege**
  3. v. 3-5: Everlasting Salvation Symbolized
     a. Golden Censer – **Prayer to God**
     b. Ark of the Covenant – **Penitence of Guilt**
        (1). The Tables of The Law
           - Represent the righteous demand of God
           - The Law Covered by Christ's Obedient Life = The Way
        (2). The Pot of Manna
           - The Satisfying of God – My Beloved Son
           - The Manna is Christ Crucified = The Truth
        (3). The Rod of Aaron that Budded
           - Christ is the light of Men = light is Life
           - The Rod is Christ's Resurrection = The Life
     c. Cherubim and The Mercy-Seat – **Presence of God**
        - The Work of Salvation Completed
- B. v. 6-10: Performance of The Services
  1. v. 6 & 10: Service of the Priest
  2. v. 7: Sacrifice for the People
  3. v. 8-9: Symbolized Pattern
- C. v. 11-15: Perfecting of Salvation
  1. v. 11-12: Come Through a Savior
  2. v. 13: Calling to Sanctification
  3. v. 14: Cleansing of the Soul
  *. v. 15: Covenant Supported
     a. Way - Death Accepted
     b. Why - Deliverance Accomplished
     c. What - Divine Assurance

****

XVI. v. 9:1-15: The Purification in
       The Lordship of Christ
   Here we will look at the model of worship based upon the Old Testament Covenant. We will also see how Christ perfected the replaced the model and gave us a new promise of the eternal inheritance.
  A. v. 1-5: Presentation of The Sanctuary
    1. v. 1: Earthly Service
      The first {or Old Testament Covenant} model of worship was based upon "divine service and an earthly sanctuary." Since this model was officiated by men it was necessary to have earthly objects to work with. In the Tabernacle {the place of worship} there were two chambers. The first was "The Holy Place" and the second was called "The Holy of Holies." Each chamber as well as the contents represented a different aspect of God's work of salvation.
    2. v. 2: Entrance to the Sanctuary {The Holy Place}
      Everything that had preceded entering into the Holy Place was preparation for the worship of God. This first chamber was the place where the worship of God was to take place. There was three pieces of furniture that was found within this chamber.
      a. Lampstand   - Potential
        The shaft, or center part, was called the candlestick. The shaft is Christ, the branches on either side are His people. Jesus in the midst. IN all things He has the pre-eminence. The branches were beaten out of it. The shaft and its branches were all of pure gold. The branches were made partakers of the same nature as the candlestick. This we, as believers, have through the operation of the Holy Spirit. Observe further that the strength of the branch lay in the shaft. Apart from the shaft the branch had no power to stand. "Without me ye can do nothing" (John 15:5). "I can do all things through Christ who strengthens me" (Philippians 4:13). The beauty of the shaft was put upon each branch. The knobs, bowls, and flowers which adorn the center

lampstand was to be wrought upon each individual branch. Is not this beautiful? Let the beauty of the Lord our God be upon us. It is the will of God that the same spirit which wrought in Jesus should work in us, changing us into the same image (2 Corinthians 3:18). Let us "put on the new man, which is after the image of Him that created him" (Col. 3:10; John 17:22). Our potential lays in Christ alone.

b. The Altar of Incense - Power through Prayer

The altar of incense must not be confused with the altar of burnt offering. No sacrifice was ever offered upon this altar. Only incense could be put upon its ever burning coals. The sacrifice must be made outside, at the door of entrance. The incense of this blood-sprinkling altar speaks of the merit of the atoning blood ascending up unto God, and may also be a foreshadowing of the precious name through which we make our requests known unto God. "If ye ask anything in My Name, I will do it" (John 14:14). "His Name is as ointment poured forth" (S of S 1:3).

The value of this altar lay in the incense. As we might expect, that which typifies the merit of God's sin-atoning Son will have something peculiar and mysterious about it. It was made by the mingling of three spices, each part was to be equal weight (Exodus 30:34-38). What these spices were no man can tell. The merit of the Lord Jesus Christ as our Redeemer consists of three parts –

1. The merit of His Life.
2. The merit of His Death.
3. The merit of His Resurrection.

These parts are all of equal weight in the sight of God. No one or two of them could avail without the other. It is a mysterious compound which only God can fully understand. He knows the value of each sweet spice.

   c. The Showbread- Privilege

The table upon which the showbread rested suggests at once the thought of fellowship. The bread was the "Bread of God," yet it was to be eaten by the priests. God and the priestly worshippers had communion and fellowship at the table. Blessed privilege, to feast on that which satisfies the heart of God. This sacred joy is ours. Christ is the "Bread of God" (Isaiah 6:33). Think of it, the holy heart of God feasting on the character and work of His Son as our Savior. He finds infinite satisfaction in Him as man's Redeemer and Representative. "This is My beloved Son, in whom I am well pleased" (Matthew 3:17). But Christ is more, He is the "Bread of Life," bread for man as well as bread for God. Wondrous grace, Christ satisfies both God and man, meets all the claims of the one, supplies all the needs of the other. At the table—in Christ as the Living Bread—we have fellowship with the Father and with His Son.

3. v. 3-5: Everlasting Salvation Symbolized

Next we enter into the Holy of Holies: Why was it called the "Holy of Holies?" It was the abode of Him who is the "holiest of all." The presence of God makes holy. The secret of all holiness is the indwelling of the holy One. It is not so much as an attainment as a possession; not so much as a rising up as a bowing down. All holiness is in God. We are holy just in proportion as we are filled with the holy One. Be filled with the Spirit, and Christ the holy One shall dwell in your heart by faith (Ephesians 3:16-17).

   a. Golden Censer – Prayer to God

When the High Priest approached the sacred place, but once a year, he came prepared: clothed in white linen robes, with shoeless feet, not without blood, and carrying the golden censer. Looking for holiness is a solemn and awful search. It is seeking to live in the light and presence of Him who tries the heart and who cannot look upon sin. It implies the concentration of all our desires into one purpose, to glorify Him (Psalm 27:4). These preparations allowed the High Priest to enter into the presence of God. Entering into the presence of God can only be accomplished after the proper preparations have been completed.

b. Ark of the Covenant – Penitence of Guilt

It is most interesting to notice that the ark was the first vessel God instructed Moses to make. In revealing this way of salvation God began with that which was nearest to Himself. How could it be otherwise if man is to be saved by grace? The first step toward redemption is a divine one. As it has been "God first" for us, so it should be "God first" in us. The ark was the center of the camp of Israel. God was in the midst of her. Jesus Christ His Son was, and is, in the midst of all God's plans and purposes. By Him God made all things: "without Him was not anything made that was made" (John 1:1-3). Through Him God made the world; through Him God also redeemed it; in all things He has the pre-eminence. Let us give Christ the high place God gives Him, the Center of all. All the other vessels in the Tabernacle were valueless without this one. They all prepared the way to this, they were but steps leading up to fellowship with God here at the mercy-seat. The Ark contained three items that picture the great salvation that is in Christ.

(1). The Tables of The Law

The law is holy, just, and good. It represents the holy and righteous demands of a just God. Even as God was placing the tablets of stone into Moses' hands it was being broken by the congregation of Israel as they danced around a golden calf. The law was broken and judgment incurred. When man failed at first God did not give him a law but a promise (Genesis 3:15). He knew that man could never be saved through law-keeping. "By the deeds of the law shall not man be justified (Romans 3:20). But now, since man has failed, grace comes in. God tells Moses to shut up the law in the ark. The ark literally kept the law. "The law was given by Moses, but grace came by Jesus Christ" (John 1:17). Christ as the ark of God could say, "Thy law have I hid in My heart, I delight to do Thy will, O my God." The holy broken law was shut up in Him. He kept it. He still keeps it. Now it is taken out of the way as an obstacle in the way of men's salvation, "Nailing it to His Cross" (Colossians 2:14). The law finds a peaceful resting-place in Him who is all glorious. It is perfectly kept here. God Himself guards it and rests satisfied on Him who covers it. Now grace reigns in righteousness.

(2). The Pot of Manna

The children of Israel fed on manna during the forty years of their wanderings. A golden pot of manna was deposited in the ark as a memorial. This was bread hidden in the ark, "Hidden manna" (Revelation 2:17). There is in Christ a secret soul-satisfying power. He is the Living Bread which came down from Heaven. The hidden bread can only be enjoyed by those who understand and appreciate a covered law. But perhaps the "hidden manna" in the ark, in which the God of glory rested, had also a heavenly aspect. Had it not a voice for God? The Lord Jesus Christ is also the "Bread of God," soul-satisfying food for the heart of His Heavenly Father. The hidden law speaks of a justice that has be satisfied, the hidden manna of a satisfied heart—"This is My beloved Son, in whom I am well pleased" (Matthew 3:17).

(3). The Rod of Aaron that Budded

The story of the rods is found in Numbers 17. The dead stick, representing Aaron, was made to bud and blossom, and bear fruit while it stood before God. The rod, then, signifies one chosen of God, One called to resurrection and life, One who was dead, but is alive again. In the ark was the rod that budded: in Christ is life for the dead.

{NOTE: In the covered law we see Christ's obedience; in the manna we see Christ's body broken for us in death; in the rod we see Christ's resurrection. The first is Christ, the Way; the second is Christ, the Truth; and the third is Christ, the Life. "I am the Way, the Truth, and the Life" (John 14:6).

  c. Cherubim and The Mercy-Seat – Presence of God

Without developing a full treatise on this subject I would present these "cherubim a representing the Church." Simply stated: Doing a comprehensive study of Ezekiel 1 & 10 one finds that the character and history of the Church of God is beautifully set forth there in these "living creatures." So here we present the cherubim on the mercy-seat, in the holy of holies, as representative of our position as "God's own within the veil, seated with Christ in heavenly places" (Ephesians 2:6). They were made out of the end of the mercy-seat, as the more literal rendering of Exodus 25:19 affirms. They were not made separately and put on the mercy-seat, but were in reality a part of it. They were both one. The mercy-seat declares God's mercy toward men through Jesus Christ, the ark on which it rested. The cherubim, or church, is connected with the mercy-seat resting on the ark of Christ's redemptive work, but linked on to God's purpose in Christ before the world began. They were made of "beaten work," wrought out by the process of beating. "Beaten work" suggests a lingering process of suffering, made through much crushing and bruising. Yes, before a Church could stand redeemed before God there must be much beating and bruising, much soul suffering and agony. Who can tell all the anguish of God while in love He gave His Son up to the death for us all. "He was wounded for our transgressions and bruised for our iniquities" (Isaiah 53:3). A saved people, a glorified Church in His own presence, will be the result of this beaten work of pure gold. Only pure gold could have stood such a

terrible test; only infinite grace could have accomplished such a work. By grace are ye saved.
B. v. 6-10: Performance of The Services
  1. v. 6 & 10: Service of the Priest
     This model of worship was conducted by the priest that had been called into service. There job was to present the sacrifices of the people to God. These sacrifices could bring relief from the guilt of sin for a season because they only dealt with "food and drinks, various washings, and fleshly ordinances imposed"
  2. v. 7: Sacrifice for the People
     Once a year the high priest went alone into the holy of holies to make atonement for the nation's sin.
  3. v. 8-9: Symbolized Pattern
     The problem with this sacrificial model of worship was that it "could not make him who performed the service perfect in regard to the conscience." This model of worship was designed to be only temporary "until the time of reformation."
C. v. 11-15: Perfecting of Salvation
  1. v. 11-12: Come Through a Savior
     For forgiveness of sins to be permanent it was necessary for a Savior to come that would replace the old style high priest whom died with a high priest whose priesthood would be continual, because He would not die. Christ became that High Priest when He offered His own blood instead of the blood of goats and calves.
  2. v. 13: Calling to Sanctification
     If the blood of animals could call people to "the purifying of the flesh" how much more can the blood of Christ call us to consecration?
  3. v. 14: Cleansing of the Soul
     You see the blood of animals may have purified the "flesh" for a time but it could not cleanse the soul. Accepting Christ blood will "cleanse your conscience from dead works to serve the living God."

*. v. 15: Covenant Supported

    This new covenant is supported in ways that the Old Testament covenant could not be. The New Testament Covenant is first supported by a Mediator {Jesus Christ} who shed His own blood and died for the sins of the people. Not only did He died but He arose on the third day to live forever more as the Mediator of this Covenant. Because Jesus is now alive He also supports this New Covenant in that His continual presence in the believer, through the power of the Holy Spirit, brings "redemption of the transgressions" that the Old Covenant could not. Finally the New Covenant is support by the fact that Christ has given us "the promise of the eternal inheritance when He promised: "Let not your heart be troubled; you believe in God, believe also in Me. In My Father's house are many mansions; if it were not so, I would have told you. I go to prepare a place for you. And if I go and prepare a place for you, I will come again and receive you to Myself; that where I am there you may be also" (John 14:1-3).

XVII. v. 9:16-28: The Quantification of
The Lordship of Christ
  A. v. 16-22: Accepted Form
    1. v. 16-17: Power of The Last Will and Testament Begun
    2. v. 18-20: Precepts of The Law Worked Through Boldly
    3. v. 21-22: Purified Legally With the Touch of Blood
  B. v. 23-26: Actual Fulfillment
    1. v. 23: Purified with Better Sacrifices
    2. v.24-26a: Presence of The Sovereign
    3. v. 26b: Putting Away of Sin
  C. v. 27-28: Appointed Future
    1. Death – Physical Death – Luke 12:20:
    2. Determination – Judgment Seat of Christ
    3. Decision – What One Believes – John 3:36:
  *. Deliverance – 1 Thess. 4:13-18 & 1 Cor. 15:51-58
  **. Dedication – "Therefore …"
    1. Comfort one another with these words."
    2. Consider – " my beloved brethren"
    3. Constant {Committed} – "be steadfast, immovable"
    4. Continuing – "always abounding in
                     the work of the Lord"
    5. Confident – "knowing that you labor
                     is not in vain in the Lord."

****

XVII. v. 9:16-28: Quantification of
              The Lordship of Christ

    To accept Jesus Christ as our Lord we must come to Christ on His terms and not ours. There is no place for someone to have a personal agenda when it comes to accepting the Lordship of Christ. We must agree to …

  A. v. 16-22: Accepted Form
    1. v. 16-17: Power of The Last Will and Testament Begun

    This concept is one that is very well understood. A last will and testament does not go into effect until after the testator had died. In most cases the contents of the last will and testament is not even known until the time of the testator's death.

2. v. 18-20: Precepts of The Law Worked Through Boldly
In the case of the Old Testament Covenant there was a necessity of a death. In this case God required that the children of Israel sacrifice animals.
3. v. 21-22: Purified Legally With the Touch of Blood
Hence, we have been given the legal requirement that blood is the price for the remission of sins and for the purifying of items that are used for the worship of God. This price was required for the Old Testament Covenant and it would be required for any new Covenant.

B. v. 23-26: Actual Fulfillment
It has been shown that all the Old Testament Worship was only a shadow of the true things that would be fulfilled in Christ. Here we see the blood covenant with God finally completed.
1. v. 23: Purified with Better Sacrifices
If it was necessary that the copies (the earthly Tabernacle model of worship) of the things in heavens should be purified with blood then it was necessary that the heavenly things be purified with "better sacrifices" than that of the blood of bulls and goats.
2. v.24-26a: Presence of The Sovereign
The "better sacrifice" was Jesus Christ Himself. On earth Jesus Christ would not have been a priest (since He was not of the tribe of Levi); therefore His sacrifice was not offered in "the holy places made with hands, which were copies of the true, but He entered into heaven itself" and presented Himself to God the Father for us.
3. v. 26b: Putting Away of Sin
The earthly sacrifices that men offered could not completely atone for the sin of men. However, Jesus "appeared to put away sin by the sacrifice of Himself." This was a sacrifice that the Father could accept as the complete atonement for the sin of mankind.

C. v. 27-28: Appointed Future
  1. Death – Physical Death – Luke 12:20:
     "But God said unto him, *Thou* fool, this night thy soul shall be required of thee: then whose shall those things be, which thou hast provided?
  2. Determination – Judgment Seat of Christ
     2 Corinthians 5:9-11 & Revelation 20:15:
     "Therefore we make it our aim, whether present or absent, to be well pleasing to Him. For we must all appear before the judgment seat of Christ, that each one may receive the things done in the body, according to what he has done, whether good or bad. And anyone not found written in the Book of Life was cast into the lake of fire." Knowing, therefore, the terror of the Lord, we persuade men …"
  3. Decision – What One Believes – John 3:36:
     "He who believes in the Son {Jesus} has everlasting life; and he who does not believe the Son shall not see life, but the wrath of God abides on him."
  *. Deliverance – 1 Thess. 4:13-18 & 1 Cor. 15:51-58
     "But I do not want you to be ignorant, brethren, concerning those who have fallen asleep, lest you sorrow as others who have no hope. For if we believe that Jesus died and rose again, even so God will bring with Him those who sleep in Jesus. For this we say to you by the word of the Lord, that we who are alive and remain until the coming of the Lord will by no means precede those who are asleep. For the Lord Himself will descend from heaven with a shout, with the voice of an archangel, and with the trumpet of God. And the dead in Christ will rise first. Then we who are alive and remain shall be changed – in a moment, in the twinkling of an eye and caught up together with them in the clouds to meet the Lord in the air. So when this corruptible has put on incorruption, and this mortal has put on immortality, then shall be brought to pass the saying that is written: Death is swallowed up in victory." O Death, where is your sting? O Hades

{grave}, where is your victory? The sting of death is sin, and the strength of sin is the law. But thanks be to God, who gives us the victory through our Lord Jesus Christ. And thus we shall always be with the Lord.

**. Dedication – "Therefore …"

These words should engender within the believer a great sense of …

1. Comfort one another with these words."

    Jesus said: "Let not your heart be troubled; you believe in God, believe also in Me. In My Father's house are many mansions; if it were not so, I would have told you. I go to prepare a place for you. And if I go and prepare a place for you, I will come again and receive you to Myself; that where I am, there you may be also" (John 14:1-3).

2. Consider – "my beloved brethren"

    "Bear one another's burdens, and so fulfill the law of Christ" (Galatians 6:2).

3. Constant {Committed} – "be steadfast, immovable"

    "But may the God of all grace, who called us to His eternal glory by Christ Jesus, after you have suffered a while, perfect, establish, strengthen, and settle you. To Him be the glory and the dominion forever and ever. Amen" (1 Peter 5:10-11).

4. Continuing – "always abounding in the work of the Lord"

    "And let us not grow weary while doing good, for in due season we shall reap if we do not lose heart. Therefore, as we have opportunity, let us do good to all, especially to those who are of the household of faith" (Galatians 6:9-10).

5. Confident – "knowing that you labor is not in vain in the Lord."

    "Do not be deceived, God is not mocked; for whatever a man sows, that he will also reap. For he who sows to his flesh will of the flesh reap corruption, but he who sows to the Spirit will of the Spirit reap everlasting life" (Galatians 6:7-8).

XVIII. v. 10:1-18: The Remission of Sins in
The Lordship of Christ
  A. v. 1-4: Shadow of Good Things to Come
    1. v. 1: Regular Services
    2. v. 2-3: Reminder of Sin
    3. v. 4: Responsibility Seen
  B. v. 5-9: Sacrifice of The Christ
    1. v. 5-7: Prophecies Outcome Arranged
    2. v. 8: Previous Offerings Adverse
    3. v. 9: Pure Obedience's Accomplishment
  C. v. 10-18: Sanctified Christian
    1. v. 10-11: Son's Sacrifice
    2. v. 12-14: Sovereign's Satisfaction
    3. v. 15-16: Spirit's Sharing
    *. v. 17-18: Saved's Salvation

****

XVIII. v. 10:1-18: The Remission of Sins in
                The Lordship of Christ

    As we came to understand in the last lesson Jesus came to fulfill the Old Testament Covenant and replace it with the New Covenant as revealed in the New Testament. The Old Testament model of worship was designed to show us our sin not to cleanse us from our sin. The Old Testament is like a mirror. We can look into it and see that we are unclean; but we cannot look into it (obey it) and be made clean.

  A. v. 1-4: Shadow of Good Things to Come
    1. v. 1: Regular Services

    The Old Testament model of worship was designed to be "a shadow of the good things to come, and not the very image of the things." Even as they fulfilled the requirements they could not be made "perfect."

    2. v. 2-3: Reminder of Sin

    Because the Old Testament sacrifices were designed to remind the participants of their need to be forgiven of their sins they had to repeat the ceremonies over and over again and year after year.

3. v. 4: Responsibility Seen

   The reason that many of the Israelites would not give up the Old Testament sacrificial system was because they had forgotten that "it is not possible that the blood of bulls and goats could take away sins. They forgot that the Law was designed to point to the coming Messiah.

B. v. 5-9: Sacrifice of The Christ

   1. v. 5-7: Prophecies Outcome Arranged

      When Christ came into the world He was fulfilling the will of God as revealed by the prophets of the Old Testament. The quoted passage here is from Psalm 40:6-8.

   2. v. 8: Previous Offerings Adverse

      God had "no pleasure in the sacrifices and offerings, burnt offerings, and offerings for sin" that "where offered according to the law" because they could not "perfect" the one's presenting the sacrifices and offerings.

   3. v. 9: Pure Obedience's Accomplishment

      Jesus' sacrifice of Himself was done in complete obedience to God's will. In Jesus' personal sacrifice the Old Testament model of the Law (the first) was taken away so that Christ could establish the New Testament model of Grace (the second).

C. v. 10-18: Sanctified Christian

   To be sanctified mean to be made clean as defined by God. An individual can be made clean because of the ...

   1. v. 10-11: Son's Sacrifice

      The Old Testament model could "never take away sins" so it was necessary for mankind to be "sanctified through the offering of the body of Jesus Christ once for all." We no longer need a earthly high priest to offer yearly sacrifices for us, which would only reminded us of our sinful natures.

2. v. 12-14: Sovereign's Satisfaction

   Jesus "offered one sacrifice for sins forever (His own body)" and then "sat down at the right hand of God." In the Tabernacle of the Old Testament there was no place for the priest to sit down. This was because their work was never done. In Jesus' case He was able to "sit down" because God accepted His offering in that it could "perfect forever those who are being sanctified."

3. v. 15-16: Spirit's Sharing

   This quote is from Jeremiah 31:33. In verses 31 and 32 we are informed that God would "make a new covenant ... not according to the covenant that was made with their fathers – the Law of Moses." The Holy Spirit gives "witness to us" in that "our body becomes the temple of the Holy Spirit who is in us, whom we have from God" (1 Corinthians 6:19). "Now he that hath wrought us for the selfsame thing is God, who also hath given unto us the earnest of the Spirit" (2 Corinthians 5:5). The Holy Spirit has been given to us as God's "earnest" (guarantee) of the future blessings that He plans to give us.

*. v. 17-18: Saved's Salvation

   In Christ we have received "remission of our sins" so there is no longer any offering for sin that is necessary. The Old Testament model of presenting a yearly sacrifice is forever ended and has become unnecessary in Jesus Christ. In Jesus Christ our "sins and our lawless deeds God will remember no longer."

XIX. v. 10:19-25: The Sanctuary (Congregational) Worship in The Lordship of Christ

<u>Intro. The Beginning of Sanctuary Worship</u>
v. 19-21

I. v. 19: Boldness of Connection Shared {in Christ's Blood}
   A. Family – "brethren"
   B. Fear of God – "having boldness to enter the Holiest"
   C. Faithful – "by the blood of Jesus"

II. v. 20: Believers Consecration Source {a new and living way}
   A. Course – "by a new and living way"
   B. Consecration – "which He consecrated for us"
   C. Conviction – "through the veil, that is, His flesh"

III. v. 21: Building of The Church Structure {the house of God}
   A. Firm Foundation – "having a High Priest"
   B. Faithful Following – "over the house of God"
   C. Fantastic Future – {implied} in what God will do for us.

****

XIX. v. 10:19-25: The Sanctuary (Congregational) Worship in The Lordship of Christ
Intro. The Beginning of Sanctuary Worship
v. 19-21

I consider this the most important aspect of being able to understand the Lordship of Christ. We are told that the Church is the body of Christ (Colossians 1:24). We are also informed that Christ is the head of the body – the Church (Colossians 1:18) and that He is also the Savior of the body – the Church (Ephesians 5:23). The New Testament Church defined is a local body of baptized believers who are associated by covenant in the faith and fellowship of the gospel: Observing the two ordinances of Christ, committed to His teachings, exercising the gifts, rights, and privileges invested in them by His Word, and seeking to extend the gospel to the ends of the earth. The word "church" is used almost every time in referring to the "local body of believers." In only three cases is the word used to refer to "every believer in the world" past and present or as some

would put it – "the universal church." We are going to look at seven aspects of how the Lordship of Christ is expressed in the Sanctuary or Congregational Worship of the Church. These are …
1. The Beliefs of the Believers
2. The Belonging of the Believers
3. The Boldness of Believers
4. The Bond of Believers
5. The Bolstering of Believers
6. The Brotherhood of Believers
7. The Building-Up of Believers

I. v. 19: Boldness of Connection Shared {in Christ's Blood}
"As many as receive Jesus Christ, to them He gives the right to become children of God, even to those who believe in His name" (John 1:12). Salvation in Jesus Christ is akin to adoption in that we become the family of God thus we are called "brethren." In this relationship we are given the right to "enter" into God's presence ("the Holiest") with boldness based upon "the blood of Jesus."

II. v. 20: Believers Consecration Source {a new and living way}
We are consecrated through "a new and living way" and not according to the Old Testament model of the law. This new way is based upon the bodily sacrifice of Jesus Christ on the cross of Calvary. When Jesus died upon the cross the "veil" of the Temple was torn from top to bottom signifying the new era. We are to live by grace and not by law.

III. v. 21: Building of The Church Structure {the house of God}
Jesus has now become our "High Priest" setting on the right hand of God making intercession for us. This "house of God" is the Church and is "built upon the foundation of the apostles and prophets, Jesus Christ Himself being the chief cornerstone, in whom the whole building being fitted together, grows into a holy temple in the Lord, in whom you also are being built together for a dwelling place of God in the Spirit" (Ephesians 2:20-22).

XIX. v. 10:19-25: The Sanctuary (Congregational) Worship in The Lordship of Christ

<u>1. The Beliefs of The Believers</u>

v. 22a

"let us draw near with a true heart in full assurance of faith"

{An Exposition Concerning
The Belief Systems of Christians}

John 8:31-32

"Then Jesus said to those Jews who believed Him,
If you abide in My word, you are My disciples indeed.
And you shall know the truth,
and the truth shall make you free."

I. Text: The Right Focus For Life
  A. They were Dedicated Because of Their Worship
    "let us draw near" & "they believed"
       The Jews mentioned here came to Jesus and believed in Him being astonished at His doctrine (Mt. 7:28; 13:54; 22:33; Mk. 1:22; 6:2; 11:18; Lk. 2:47; 4:32;).
  B. They were Disciples Because of The Word
    "with a true heart" & "they continued in the word"
       They became Jesus' disciples because they were doers of the Word and not hearers only.
  C. They were Delivered Because of His Witness
    "in full assurance of faith" &
    "they knew the truth, and the truth set them free"
       Truth is from God. When one accepts the truth (not merely man's ideas of what is truth) then real freedom is attained.
II. 2 Timothy 2:15: The Right Flavor For Life
    "Study to be approved of God"
       If life is to be worth living one is encouraged to "study" the things of God. In Acts 17:11 The Bareans where considered "more fair-minded than those in Thessalonica, in that they received the Word with all readiness, and <u>searched the Scriptures daily</u> to find out whether these things were so." By diligently studying the Scriptures and applying them to life we will be …

A. Christian in our Doings
   "a workman"
   We have been "created in Christ Jesus for good works, which God prepared beforehand that we should walk in them" (Ephesians 2:10). In this we are to "let our light (Christian witness) shine before men, that they may see our good works and glorify our Father in heaven" (Matthew 5:16).
B. Courageous in our Defense
   "not ashamed"
   We are encouraged to study God's Word so that we can "always be ready to give a defense to everyone who asks us a reason for the hope that is in us, with meekness and fear; having a good conscience, that when they defame us as evildoers, those who revile our good conduct in Christ may be ashamed" (1 Peter 3:15-16).
C. Confirmed in our Doctrine
   "rightly discerning (understanding) the word of truth"
   Having taken the time to properly study the Scriptures one has the ability to understand its meaning. The idea here is that rightly dividing the word of truth, is to understand it and continue in the true doctrine by actions, and teaching that truth to every person.
III. 2 Timothy 3:14-17: The Right Foundation For Life
   We should understand that the Scriptures properly understood are the Right Foundation For Life. Life based upon any other belief system will fail in the end. The Scriptures give us four things:
   *. v. 14: Intro. Good Building Blocks
               Provide Required Training
   1. Consistent – "continue thou in the things"
   2. Cultivated – "which thou has learned"
   3. Certain – "and have been assured of"
      When the Scriptures are used as the basis for life it gives and individual the right building blocks for a productive life. The right building blocks require will lead one to receive the required training for life. This

training should be consistent in that it is unchanging no matter what the situation is. This training must be cultivated in that it is to be learned. People do not naturally know these spiritual details. This spiritual training also must be "certain" in that it has been confirmed by the Christian community as real because it is "the things which have been learned and received and heard and seen lived out" (Philippians 4:9) in the lives of God's people. It is not some "new" doctrine that is opposed to the Christian heritage that has already been acknowledged that is from God. Paul gives warning not to be "turned away from Him who called you in the grace of Christ, to a different gospel, which is not another; but there are some who trouble you and want to pervert the gospel of Christ. As we have said before, so now I say again, if anyone preaches any other gospel to you than what you have received let him be accursed" (Galatians 1:7 & 9).

A. v. 15: Good Background
Promotes Right Thinking

When an individual begins with a good background of knowledge proper thinking becomes easy. The opposite is also true: when an individual begins with a bad background of knowledge wrong and improper thinking become the norm for one's life. Therefore having a good background of knowledge is advantageous for right thinking.

1. Aware – "and from a child you have known the Holy Scriptures"

Timothy had been aware of the Holy Scriptures from his early childhood. He probably grew up have memorized much of the Scriptures as a young man. Not everyone has had this privilege; but for those that have it is of a great advantage.

2. Acknowledge – "which are able to make you wise unto salvation"

   The purpose of the Holy Scriptures is to reveal to mankind the nature of God. Jesus Himself said that He had come to show us the Father. By knowing God mankind is given the opportunity to receive salvation.

3. Accept – "through faith which is in Christ Jesus"

   This salvation is found in having a right relationship with Christ Jesus. For "whoever transgresses and does not abide in the doctrine of Christ does not have God. He who abides in the doctrine of Christ has both the Father and the Son" (2 John 9).

B. v. 16: Good Basics are Profitable For Rigorous Truth

   It is vital to have good basics when it comes to having correct truth. If one begins with wrong preconceptions or preconceived ideas then their conclusions will be erroneous and misleading. The Holy Scripture is the best place to begin when seeking the Truth because "all Scripture is given by inspiration of God, and is profitable for …

1. Belief System – "doctrine"

   Many rebel at the word "doctrine." Properly understood we recognize that the word simply means "what one believes and basis their life upon." The Bible and its teachings is the best place to begin building a belief system upon which one can construct a productive and happy life.

2. Betterment – "for reproof, for correction"

   The Bible is also a great place to learn what constitutes wrong and right behavior. The world's standard of right and wrong behavior is in constant flux. A standard of right and wrong behavior based upon a right understanding of God's Word is consistent. The Bible is profitable "for reproof": This means that the Word of God will inform us of what is wrong and unacceptable behavior. The bible is profitable "for correction": This means that the Word of God will inform us of how to correct the wrong or unacceptable behavior. The Bible does not just inform about what it wrong, it also informs us how to correct the wrong. God's Word not only deals with behavior it also deals with how to know what is right or wrong

3. Basic Understanding – "for instruction in righteousness"

The Holy Scripture is also profitable for "instruction in righteousness" or having a right understanding of what the standard of God is for righteousness. Right and wrong is not determined by what mankind accepts as right or wrong. Jesus Christ is the ultimate standard of right and wrong. In John chapter one we are informed that Jesus is the "light which shines in the darkness (the world), and the darkness (world) understood Him not" (John 1:1-5). Jesus tells us that "this is the condemnation, that the light has come into the world, and men loved darkness rather than light, because their deeds were evil. For everyone practicing evil hates the light and does not come to the light, lest his deeds should be exposed. But he who does the truth comes to the light, that his deeds may be clearly seen, that they have been done in God" (John 3:19-20). To know what is right or wrong one must know Jesus Christ and what His Word teaches.

C. v. 17: Good Beliefs are

Productive of Righteous Transactions

If an individual has good beliefs then that individual will have a life which is modeled after Jesus Christ. The Holy Bible has been given to mankind "that the child of God may be ..."

1. Perfect – "may be perfect" {matured}

It is the will of God that each Christian comes to a place of spiritual maturity. Peter gives us a clue to this spiritual growth by encouraging Christians to "give all diligence to add to our faith: virtue, knowledge, self-control, perseverance, godliness, brotherly kindness, and love" (2 Peter 1:5-7). Peter then informs us that if an individual "has these qualities in abundance that one

will be neither barren nor unfruitful in the knowledge of our Lord Jesus Christ" (1 Peter 1:8).
2. Prepared – "thoroughly furnished"

The child of God whom has applied the Holy Scriptures to their life will have everything that is needful to live a life for God. One aspect of applying the Word of God to one's life is by "Putting on the whole armor of God, that you may be able to stand against the wiles of the devil" (Ephesians 6:11). The soldier of Christ must therefore be … (study of Ephesians 6:14-18 →

   (1). v. 14-15: Determined to Stand
     (a). Right –
     "girded with the truth"
     (b). Righteousness of Heart –
     "breastplate of righteousness"
     (c). Religious Training
     "shod feet with the preparation of the gospel of peace"
   (2). v. 16-17: Defensively Sheltered
     (a). Pleasing to God
     "the shield of faith"
     (b). Protection we Need
     "helmet of salvation"
     (c). Power of The Word
     "the sword of the Spirit = the Word of God"
   (3). v. 18: Develop Spiritually
     (a). Spiritual Source
     "praying always with all prayer and supplication in the Spirit"
     (b). Steadfast Sight
     "watchful to this end with all perseverance"
     (c). Seeking for the Saints (The Church)
     "and supplication for all the saints"

By putting into practice God's Word a Christian will have all the necessary equipment needed to live a life pleasing unto our Lord and Savior Jesus Christ.

3. Practiced – "unto all good works"

    Although good works does not save an individual, good works is a normal and natural outcome of accepting Jesus Christ as one's personal Savior and Lord. Someone whom has been saved by grace through faith in Jesus Christ is become "God's workmanship, created in Christ Jesus for good works, which God prepared beforehand that we should walk in them" (Ephesians 2:9-10).

John R. W. Scott has written:

    "The secrets of Christian maturity are to be found in Scriptures by all who seek them. There is a breadth of God's word which few of us ever encompass, a depth which we seldom reach. The Bible is the portrait of Jesus Christ. We need to gaze upon Him with such intensity of desire that (by the gracious work of the Holy Spirit) He come alive to us, meets us, and fills us with Himself."

Augustine put it this way:

    "Ignorance of Scripture is ignorance of Christ."

XIX. v. 10:19-25: The Sanctuary (Congregational) Worship in The Lordship of Christ

<u>2. The Belonging of Believers</u>
v. 22b:
"having our hearts sprinkled from an evil conscience
and our bodies washed with pure water."

When one studies "Baptism" their belief concerning the nature of Salvation must first be considered. If one believes that baptism is necessary for salvation to be accomplished their view of baptism itself is changed. One who believes that "by grace one has been saved through faith, and that not of themselves, it is the gift of God, not of works, lest anyone should boast and that Christians are God's workmanship, created in Christ Jesus for good works, which God prepared beforehand that they should be accomplished in them" (Ephesians 2:8-10) also has a specific view of baptism. This view of baptism is what will be shared here. This study is not specifically designed to argue the point; however, here is presented an in-depth look at baptism as a symbol of salvation that has been already accomplished through faith in Jesus Christ.

A Theological Look at Baptism
Romans 6:3-4, 22-23
Romans 5:17-18, 21
Galatians 2:20

As we give consideration to the doctrine of baptism we are going to look at the need for salvation, salvation itself, the symbolism of baptism, the evidence of the new life in Christ, and the idea of being new in Christ.

I. v. 5:17-18, 21: Theology of The Belief About Sin

There are those today that would scoff at the idea of "sin." They think that the idea of "sin" is silly. Part of the reason that they do so is because if they admit that "sin" is real they also have to admit that God is real. Evil actions are against people and harm people but "sin" is against God and God alone as David confessed:

"For I acknowledge my transgressions and my sin is always before me. Against You and You only, have I sinned, and done this evil in Your sight" (Psalm 51:3-4). Let us look at the problem of sin.

A. Imparted Sin – death
  1. Guiding Act –
    "by one man's offense death reigned"

    Why is there death in the world? The answer to this important question is found in the first book of the Bible. God created the cosmos in seven literal days. In the creative acts of God, He created man and woman (Adam and Eve). God placed Adam and Eve in a garden and gave them charge over keeping the garden. There was one command given to Adam and Eve and that command was: "Of every tree of the garden you may freely eat; but of the tree of the knowledge of good and evil you shall not eat, for in the day that you eat of it you shall surely die" (Genesis 2:16-17). Because Adam disobeyed God death entered into the realm of the cosmos (the creation of God).

  2. Guilty Association –
    "by one man's offense judgment came to all men"

    Some have questioned: Since it was Adam that sinned why do we bear the judgment of death that was placed upon him? The answer is very simple: we receive from our ancestors the qualities that make us human. One of those qualities is that we have a sinful nature and "thus death spread to all men, because all sinned" (Romans 5:12).

  3. Grievous Action –
    "sin reigned in death"

    The result of sin was and is death. Death was not in God's plan for man. Having given man free will though, sin became an interruption in the workings of mankind. In His foreknowledge God planned "before the foundation of the world" to redeem mankind from his sin because He knew man would sin before He created Him.

B. Imputed righteousness – "forgiveness"
 1. Righteousness Given by one Man
    Just as sin was passed to mankind by the act of one man (Adam) righteousness is given by one Man (Jesus Christ) as the gift of grace. We understand that the sinful nature of man prevents man from coming to God on his own. Therefore, by the grace of God, the Holy Spirit draws individuals to the only one that is capable of imparting righteousness because He {Jesus} "was tempted in all manner as we were yet without sin" (Hebrews 4:15).
 2. Reason for Living
    By one Man's righteous act, the free gift came to all men = justification of life. It was by death on the cross that Christ shed His blood to bring us redemption and forgiveness for our sin.
 3. Required Purity
    You should know as a Christian "that your body is the temple of the Holy Spirit who is in you, whom you have from God, and you are not your own. For you were bought at a price; therefore glorify God in your body and in your spirit, which are God's" (1 Corinthians 6:19-20). Live based upon His leading and in so doing grace will reign through righteousness as you live for Him.
C. Inclusive Grace = Eternal Life
 1. The One –
    Forgiveness {thus salvation} is only possible through the One = Jesus Christ. "Neither is there salvation in any other: for there is none other name under heaven given among men, whereby we must be saved" (Acts 4:12). "For *there is* one God, and one mediator between God and men, the man Christ Jesus" (1 Timothy 2:5).

2. The Offer –
    The free gift has been offered by "God our Savior; Who will have all men to be saved, and to come unto the knowledge of the truth " (1 Timothy 2:3-4). "God so loved the world that He gave His only begotten Son, that whoever believes in Him should not perish but have everlasting life. For God did not send His Son into the world to condemn the world, but that the world through Him might be saved" (John 3:16-17).
3. The Opportunity –
    The question was given: "What must I do to be saved?" They answer was "Believe on the Lord Jesus Christ, and you will be saved" (Acts 16:30-31). "He who believes in Jesus is not condemned; but he who does not believe is condemned already, because he has not believed in the name of the only begotten Son of God. And this is the condemnation, that the light has come into the world, and men loved darkness rather than light, because their deeds were evil. For everyone practicing evil hates the light and does not come to the light, lest his deeds should be exposed. But he who does the truth comes to the light, that his deeds may be clearly seen, that they have been done in God" (John 3:13-21). Salvation has been offered through the Lord Jesus Christ to those whom chose to accept His forgiveness for their sin.

II. v. 6:3-4: Theology of Baptism as a Symbol
    Understanding that salvation is through Jesus, "the author and finisher of our faith" (Hebrews 12:2) we realize that baptism is a picture of what has already happened in the heart of the believer.

A. Church Membership in Christ's Body
    "as many as of us were baptized **into** Christ Jesus"
    = The Church is the Body of Christ (Colossians)
    Here we are told that when one is baptized they are baptized INTO Christ Jesus. This begs the question: What does "into Christ Jesus" mean? Paul states in Colossians 1:24: "I now rejoice in my sufferings for

you, and fill up in my flesh what is lacking in the afflictions of Christ, for the sake of His body, which is the church." The Scriptures also refer to "Christ as the Head of the body." We understand this is symbolism, but none the less we must accept it as accurate. Hence we also understand the symbolism of baptism in that one is "baptized into Christ Jesus" that one is baptized in the "body of Christ" = The Church. Therefore it is by the act of baptism that one is recognized as being part of the Church = becoming an active member of a local body of baptized believers which have covenanted together for the furtherance of the Gospel of Jesus Christ.

B. Correct {only} Mode of Christian Baptism

"we were **buried** with Him through baptism into death"

"What is the correct mode of Christian baptism?" Many have asked this question over the years. Some groups have used sprinkling as a method, some have used pouring as a method and some may have used a combination of these two. I suggest that the question is flawed. The question implies that there may be many methods of baptism. This is obviously wrong when one takes the time to look at this Scripture passage. There is only one method of baptism which would symbolize an individual being "buried with Christ unto His death." That method is Full Emersion. Baptism is to symbolize the death, the burial, and the resurrection of Christ. Only by full emersion can this be pictured.

C. Creation Made by "Christ Belief" – 2 Cor. 5:17

"Therefore, if anyone is in Christ, he is a new creation; old things have passed away; behold, all things have become new."

To give emphasis to the fact that baptism cannot save we must understand that salvation is accomplished when one accepts Christ in the free pardon of sin that is offered by the shed blood of the cross of Calvary. This New Life is lived in Christ because it is Christ Himself which creates that newness.

III. Galatians 2:20: Theology of a Believable Salvation

When an individual accepts the new life which Christ offers that one's life is changed! Paul describes the attributes of this change.

  A. Decision – "Bear our Cross"

"I have been crucified with Christ"

The first attribute of believable Christianity is one of intentional purpose. In Luke 9:23 Jesus said: "If anyone desires to come after Me, let him deny himself, and take up his cross daily, and follow Me." Jesus teaches us that there are four qualities of a decision to follow Him:

    1. Desire – "if anyone desires to come after Me"
    2. Denial of Self – "let him deny himself"
    3. Daily Discipline – "take up his cross daily"
    4. Directional Purpose – "and follow Me"

Once Christ has become Savior and Lord this one will have begun the process of "being crucified with Christ."

  B. Dedication – Belong to Christ

"it is no longer I who lives, but Christ lives in me"

After one has honestly made the decision to follow Christ and the new birth has taken place that one will dedicate himself or herself to living for Christ. "He who is called while free is Christ's slave. For we were bought at a price" (1 Corinthians 7:22-23).

  C. Direction – Belief Character

"and the life which I now live in the flesh I live by faith in the Son of God, who loves me and gave Himself for me."

The Christian has had their character changes in Christ. "Those who are Christi's have crucified the flesh with its passions and desires. If we live in the Spirit, let us also walk in the Spirit. Let us not become conceited, provoking one another, or envying one another" (Galatians 5:24-26).

IV. v. 6:22a-c: Theology of Being Saved

You must understand that "to whom you present yourselves slaves to obey, you are that one's slaves whom you obey, whether of sin leading to death, or of obedience leading to righteousness" (Romans 6:16). Every person is a slave to someone (God or the devil). Every person has already made that choice. Now the choice can be changed, but understand that everyone is slave to someone. As Believers in Christ we are …

A. Set-Free from Sin

"and having been set free from sin"

Does being set free from sin mean that one will never commit another sin as long as they live? A resounding No is the answer. "We know that Jesus was manifested to take away our sins, and in Him there is no sin. Therefore whoever abides in Jesus does not continue to live in sin" (1 John 3:5-6). A born again individual is no longer a slave to sin; even though an individual temptation may lead one to commit a sinful act. Paul expressed it this way: "For we know that the law is spiritual: but I am carnal, sold under sin. For that which I do I allow not: for what I would, that do I not; but what I hate, that do I. If then I do that which I would not, I consent unto the law that *it is* good. Now then it is no more I that do it, but sin that dwelleth in me. For I know that in me (that is, in my flesh,) dwelleth no good thing: for to will is present with me; but *how* to perform that which is good I find not. For the good that I would I do not: but the evil which I would not, that I do. Now if I do that I would not, it is no more I that do it, but sin that dwelleth in me. I find then a law, that, when I would do good, evil is present with me. For I delight in the law of God after the inward man: But I see another law in my members, warring against the law of my mind, and bringing me into captivity to the law of sin which is in my members. O wretched man that I am! who shall deliver me from the body of this death? I thank God through Jesus

Christ our Lord. So then with the mind I myself serve the law of God; but with the flesh the law of sin" (Romans 7:14-25).
- B. Servant to our Savior
"having become slaves of God"
The child of God becomes the willing slave to our Lord and Savior Jesus Christ. We desire to be obedient and in the end to stand before Jesus and hear Him say to us: "Well done, good and faithful servant; you have been faithful over a few things, I will make you ruler over many things. Enter into the joy of your Lord" (Matthew 25:23).
- C. Seen Salvation
"you have your fruit to holiness"
"The fruit of the Spirit is love, joy, peace, longsuffering, kindness, goodness, faithfulness, gentleness, self-control, Against such there is no law" (Galatians 5:22-23). True Christianity is obvious. We do our "good works that men may see them and glorify our Father which is in heaven" (Matthew 5:16).

V. v. 6:22d-23: Theology of Being

Since Christianity is obvious let us understand the Christian's ...

- A. Goal – "and the end, everlasting life"
Jesus pointed out our goal when He said to His disciples: "Let not your heart be troubled; you believe in God, believe also in Me. In My Father's house are many mansions; if it were not so, I would have told you. I go to prepare a place for you. And if I go and prepare a place for you, I will come again and receive you to Myself; that where I am, there you may be also. And where I go you know, and the way you know. ... I am the Way, the Truth, and the Life. No one comes to the Father except through Me" (John 14:1-4, 6).

B. Grief – "for the wages of sin is death"
   Those whom refuse to accept the gospel of Jesus Christ grieve the Christian. We with God would have "all men to be saved and come to the knowledge of the truth" (1 Timothy 2:4).
C. Gift – "but the gift of God is eternal life" in
   We recognize that the only way to have a right relationship with God is to have a right relationship with Christ Jesus our Lord.
   1. Personal Newness of The Gift – "Christ" = Messiah
      Jesus is God's Messiah. The plan of salvation that one must follow to be forgiven of their sin is the plan that God created before the foundation of the world was laid. No one can come to God based upon the own personal agenda.
   2. Personal Nature of The Gift – "Jesus" = Maker/Creator
      The nature of the gift of salvation is based in the fact that God Himself came to pay the price necessary to pay the wages of sin – death, even death on the cross. God knew that we owed a debt that we could never pay: so God paid the debt that He did no owe that we might be forgiven and come into a right relationship with Him.
   3. Personal Need of The Gift – "our Lord" = Our Making
      Every person has the need for this gift of salvation because "all have sinned and fallen short of the glory of God" (Romans 3:23). The best morality that men can offer is "as an unclean *thing*, and all our righteousnesses *are* as filthy rags; and we all do fade as a leaf; and our iniquities, like the wind, have taken us away" (Isaiah 64:6).

XIX. v. 10:19-25: The Sanctuary (Congregational) Worship in The Lordship of Christ

3. v. 23: The Boldness of Believers

"Let us hold fast the confession of our hope
without wavering, for He who promised is faithful."

The command to "hold fast the confession of our hope without wavering" is a command to give a strong …

DEFENSE of Our Faith

1 Peter 3:15-16:

"Sanctify the Lord God in your hearts, and always be ready to give a defense to everyone who asks you a reason for the hope that is in you, with meekness and fear; having a good conscience, that when they defame you as evildoers, those who revile your good conduct in Christ may be ashamed."

As a Christians serve the Lord God with their whole hearts they can be ready to defend their faith in Jesus Christ as the only way of salvation to those who ask a reason for the hope they is seen in the Christian's life. This encouragement implies that the Christian is living in such a way that the individuals around will see in them things which point to Jesus Christ. Because of what they see in the life of the Christian they will ask about their hope which is founded in Jesus Christ. Paul mentions seven characteristics which every Christian should model to show others that they are living in the hope based upon the resurrection of Jesus Christ and the promises that Christians have because of their faith.

DISCERNMENT OF CHARACTER

2 Timothy 3:10

"But you have carefully followed my doctrine, manner of life, purpose, faith, longsuffering, love, perseverance."

"But thou hast fully known my ..."
1. DOCTRINE – "doctrine" – John 6:69
"And we believe and are sure that thou (Jesus) art the Christ, the Son of the Living God."

The basic belief of a Christian is that Jesus is the Christ, the Son of the Living God. The only way to a right relationship with God the Father is to have a right relationship with Jesus Christ as one's personal Savior and Lord. To reject Jesus is to reject the plan of salvation that God Himself has put into operation. The Holy Bible as interpreted by Jesus Christ is the authority by which the Christian determines what is right or what is wrong. It has been understood in all Christian tradition that we must allow "Scripture to interpret Scripture" for no Scriptures is of any private interpretation. It does matter what one believes and how that one has come to that belief. There are proper rules of interpreting language and the written word. There are also proper rules of interpreting the Bible. Although not exhaustive, the following are a few rules of proper interpretation:

(1). Divinely Inspired

We must accept that the Bible is divinely inspired by God as He used people to record His message. God is the author of the Bible even though it was humanly pinned and humanly preserved.

(2). Understanding What the Writer Meant

An honest evaluation of what was meant when the writer wrote the passage gives us a basic correct understanding of what we are to learn from a passage.

(3). Passage Interpreted in Context

Verses of Scripture cannot be pulled out of their framework to force a meaning from them. The meaning must make sense with the surrounding verses.

(4). Environment of the Author
   When and where did the author live and what was the cultural surroundings that he was familiar with.
(5). To Whom was It Written
   What was the background and surroundings of those whom would be reading the Scriptures? How would they have understood the words?
(6). Literary Type
   The type of literature that the passage is important in understanding its meaning: is the passage narrative, poetry, history, informative, or ect.
(7). Generally – each statement has one Meaning
   Don't try to force multiple meanings upon a passage of Scripture
(8). Miracles – secured contact with the World – & Why It was Performed
   The Bible must be accepted as a "supernatural book" dealing with Spiritual things. Don't deny something simply because you don't understand it or because it is hard to believe.
(9). Parables – Generally Conveyed one Message
   Be careful not to allegorize parables to a point beyond what they are meant to teach.
(10). Bible – Is A Book of Faith
   Remember the Bible's primary purpose is to reveal God and His plan of salvation through Jesus Christ to mankind. Even though it is not a science book it is correct in the science that it reveals; though it is not a history book it is correct in the history that it reveals; though it is not a geology book it is correct in the geology that it reveals: It

is a Book of Religion and it reveals how we as men can know God.
- (11). In Harmony with the tone of the whole Bible

    The interpretation of a passage of Scripture must be in character with the attitude of the whole Bible. If a belief differs from the spirit of the entire Bible then that belief is wrong. God's Word is of a unique unity in its teachings.
- (12). Depend on the Holy Spirit

    Remember that for the Christian the Holy Spirit is our Teacher. We must depend upon Him to lead us to a proper understanding of God's Word. But always remember that Jesus informed us that the teaching of the Holy Spirit would always glorify Jesus Christ.

2. DESIGN – "manner of life" – Philippians 1:27

"Only let your lifestyle be as it becomes the Gospel of Christ: that whether I come and see you, or else be absent, I may hear of your affairs, that you stand fast in one spirit, with one mind striving together for the faith of the Gospel;"

The way that a Christian conducts his life is very important in being a witness for Jesus Christ. "Whatever you do in word or deed, do all in the name of the Lord Jesus, giving thanks to God the Father through Him" (Colossians 3:17). We have been called to "be the light of the world." We are to "let out light shine, like a city set upon a hill which cannot be hid, before men that they may see our good works and glorify our Father which is in heaven" (Matthew 5:14-16). Our lives are to give evidence that the Gospel of Jesus Christ is real and that it is the only way to a right relationship with God.

3. DESIRE – purpose – 1 Timothy 2:3-4

"For this is good and acceptable in the sight of God our Savior: Who will have all men to be saved, and come to the knowledge of the truth."

The Philippian Church was encouraged to "be likeminded, having the same love, being of one accord, of one mind. Let nothing be done through selfish ambition or conceit, but in lowliness of mind let each esteem others better than himself. Let each of you look out not only for his own interests, but also for the interest of other. Let this mind be in you which was also in Christ Jesus" (Philippians 2:2-5). The Christian's purpose in life should be to see others come to know Jesus Christ as Savior and Lord.

4. DISCIPLESHIP – faith – Luke 9:23

"And Jesus said unto them all, If any man will come after me, let him deny himself, and take up his cross daily, and follow me."

1. Desire – "if anyone desires to come after Me"
2. Denial of Self – "let him deny himself"
3. Daily Discipline – "take up his cross daily"
4. Directional Purpose – "and follow Me"

Our faith in Jesus Christ is developing faith. It begins with a decision to accept Jesus Christ as the only way of salvation. This positive decision will lead one to deny their worldly lusts and strive to follow the teachings of Jesus. That individual will realize that living for Jesus involves a daily commitment to being obedient to the leadership of God through the Holy Spirit. Having made these decisions this individual will have a specific direction for their life ("follow Jesus"). The Scriptural word for discipleship is "sanctification." Simply put: this means spiritual growth.

5. DEDICATION – longsuffering – 1 Peter 4:16

"Yet if any man suffer as a Christian, let him not be ashamed; but let him glorify God on this behalf."

There is a popular teaching today which says that if an individual is a Christian in right relationship with

God that one will have no problems and will always be financially independent. Although this is a great sounding statement it is just not true based upon what the Bible informs us that Jesus taught His followers. Jesus said that in this would you would have tribulation. Jesus invited people to: "Come unto me, all *ye* that labor and are heavy laden, and I will give you rest. Take my yoke upon you, and learn of me; for I am meek and lowly in heart: and ye shall find rest unto your souls. For my yoke *is* easy, and my burden is light" (Matthew 11:28-30). Jesus did not say that He would remove all burdens. He said that He would take away the burdens of the world and replace them with His "yoke which is easy and with His burden which is light." As it says in the book of Job: "Day of man born to woman are short and full of trouble." For the Christian this truth is compounded with the fact that Jesus informed us "That the world hated Him and it would also hate us." The faithful Christian will suffer for Christ in a world that rejects Jesus as the only way of salvation.

6. DEVOTION – love – 1 Corinthians 13:13

"And now abides faith, hope and love, these three; but the greatest of these is love."

The devotion which keeps the Christian stable in a world of tribulation is three-fold. The connection of these three is seen in our "being justified by faith, we have peace with God through our Lord Jesus Christ: By whom also we have access by faith into this grace wherein we stand, and rejoice in hope of the glory of God. And not only *so*, but we glory in tribulations also: knowing that tribulation works patience; and patience, experience; and experience, hope: And hope makes not ashamed; because the love of God is shed abroad in our hearts by the Holy Ghost which is given unto us" Romans 5:1-5).

7. DURABILITY – perseverance – 1 John 5:4-5

"For whatsoever is born of God overcomes the world: and this is the victory that overcomes the world, even our faith. Who is he that overcomes the world, but he that believes that Jesus is the Son of God."

John also refers to this victory in the gospel that he wrote. In John 1:13 he gives us the Pattern of Faith: One …

  a. cannot Inherit It – "not of blood"

  This victorious faith is not merely a belief system that is passed down through families. Although the Christian faith is to be shared with one's family, as commanded by God, just believing "about" God and Jesus is not enough. Being born into a "Christian Family" does not secure one's place in the family of God.

  b. cannot Invoke It –"not of the flesh"→not by men

  Mankind does not have it within himself to be able to qualify worthy of receiving salvation from God. Scripture informs us that our moral best is as "filthy rags" before a perfect, righteous, and holy God. Neither can man purchase salvation through material or financial means. Salvation is not within the grasp of man left to himself.

  c. cannot Insist on It – "not of the will"

  Also man does not have the option of deciding when and where he will accept the offer of salvation in Jesus Christ. One may refuse the offer of salvation choosing to wait for a future time to accept the opportunity which may never arise. One such obstacle to a future acceptance is the interruption of death.

*. it is by Invitation Only – "of God"
> This victorious faith is by invitation only for we are told by Jesus in John 6:44: "No man can come to me, except the Father which hath sent me draw him: and I will raise him up at the last day." Because of man's sinful nature, man left to himself, would never seek a relationship with God through Jesus Christ. Therefore it takes the conviction of God through the power of the Holy Spirit for one to come to Jesus Christ for salvation.

Therefore when one comes to God through Jesus Christ that individual receives the ability to overcome the world. The things that we can and will overcome in the world are found in Romans 8:35 & 37: "Who shall separate us from the love of Christ? Shall tribulation, or distress, or persecution, or famine, or nakedness, or peril, or sword? Nay, in all these things we are more than conquerors through Him that loved us." The areas of overcoming are:
1. Problems = "tribulation"
2. Pain = "distress"
3. Persecution
4. Pestilence = "famine"
5. Poverty = "nakedness"
6. Peril – (danger)
7. Pressure = "sword"

In all these areas we are more than conquerors through our Lord and Savior Jesus Christ. None of these things can separate us from the love of Jesus and as He makes us "new creations in Him" we can overcome the world by our faith in Him.

XIX. v. 10:19-25: The Sanctuary (Congregational) Worship in The Lordship of Christ
4. v. 24a: The Bond of Believers
"Let us consider one another in order to stir up love"

When asked by a scribe: "Which is the first commandment of all?" Jesus answered him, "The first of all the commandments *is: 'Hear, O Israel, the Lord our God, the Lord is one. And you shall love the Lord your God with all your heart, with all your soul, with all your mind, and with all your strength.'* This *is* the first commandment. And the second, like *it, is* this: *'You shall love your neighbor as yourself.'* There is no other commandment greater than these" (Mark 12:28-31). Jesus placed a great emphasis upon love. As His followers we must also place great importance upon love. Let us look at …

5 NOTIONS ABOUT LOVE
1 Corinthians 13:1-13

I. v. 1-3: **NECESSITY** of Love
  A. v. 1: To be a SPEAKER is not enough
    - the use of the Tongue
    1. Eloquent – Without Love
      "though I speak with the tongues of men"
    2. Evangelical – Without Love
      "though I speak with the tongues … of angels"
    3. Empty – Without Love
      "as a sounding brass, or a tinkling cymbal"

      The Bible speaks much about the use of the tongue. James warns us that "no man can tame the tongue. It is an unruly evil, full of deadly poison. With it we bless our God and Father, and with it we curse men, who have been made in the similitude of God. Out of the same mouth proceed blessing and cursing. My brethren, these things ought not to be so" (James 3:8-10). Paul here informs us that no matter how eloquent or evangelical a person may be if they speak without love that individual is empty and his speech is empty of value.

B. v. 2: To be SPIRITUAL is not enough
    - the use of Talents
  1. To Impart Wisdom
    "prophecy, understanding, knowledge"
  2. To Increase Worship
    "have all faith"
  3. To Ineffective Witness
    "and have not love"

    Jesus taught much about using the abilities that God has given us for the Kingdom work of God. Each individual has talents and gifts that can be used to spread the gospel of Jesus Christ. We must understand that when we use the natural talents that we have been born with or the special gifts that God has imparted to us to further the cause of Christ it must been done in love for those whom we are working with. Without genuine love our witness for Christ becomes ineffective and false. This leads to hypocrisy.

C. v. 3: To be a SHARER is not enough
    - the use of the Tithe & Offering
  1. Sacrifice to Feed
    "though I bestow all my goods to feed the poor"
  2. Suffer for the Faith
    "and though I give my body to be burned"
  3. Sham without Love of the Father
    "and have not love, it profits me nothing"

    God also blesses individuals with material and financial resources to be used for the Kingdom work of Christ. When these resources are used to help share Jesus Christ with the needy it will profit nothing for the individual doing the sharing if it is done without love. Notice that Paul does not say that it will not profit those being helped. The recipients of the goods will be better off for the deed even if the sharer receives no benefit from the transaction.

II. v. 4-6: **NURTURE** of Love

    When an individual has the love of God dwelling within them it will be noticed in one's spirit, body, and soul.

  A. v. 4: ATTITUDE of Love

    The love of God within one will be seen in one's sprit (the character of an individual). God's love in one causes that individual to be …

    1. Hospitable

    "love suffers long and is kind"

    Patience grows from the influence of God's love upon one's life. This patience with others will allow one to treat others with kindness even when they do not deserve it.

    2. Honest

    "love envies not"

    Envy is born out of a dishonest spirit. When one fills that they deserve what others have resentment and hatred begin to grow. A honest spirit is content with the blessings of God in their life and does not base happiness upon the things that they possess.

    3. Humble

    "love vaunts not itself, is not puffed up"

    Dwelling in God's love helps in "not thinking more highly of ourselves than we ought to think" (Romans 12:3). We realize that not only without Christ we can do nothing (John 15:5) but also that without Christ we are nothing.

  B. v. 5a-b: ACTION of Love

    The love of God within oneself will be seen in one's body (the course of an individual). God's love in one causes that individual to be …

    1. Proper

    "love does not behave itself unseemly"

    Christians should act like Christians. This on the surface may sound like a naive statement; nevertheless I still believe that it is true. When Christians act unchristian and immoral they are not living in the love

of God. God's love produces gentle actions in those controlled by it.
2. Preferential
"love seeks not her own"
Where God's love is there can never be selfishness. Love looks to the needs of others and is concerned with how to help others find God in the free pardon of sin that is offered through Jesus Christ. Love will seek to do what is necessary to show others the way of the cross.
3. Peacemaker
"love is not easily provoked"
Love seeks "if it is possible, as much as depends on us, to live peaceably with all men" (Romans 12:18). James encourages "my beloved brethren, let every man be swift to hear, slow to speak, slow to wrath; for the wrath of man does not produce the righteousness of God" James 1:19-20).

C. v. 5c-6: ACCEPTANCE of Love
The love of God within one will be seen in one's soul (the conscience of an individual). God's love in one causes that individual to be …
1. Righteous
"thinks no evil"
. Realizing that within mankind "there is none who does good, no, not one" (Romans 3:12) love still seeks to find "good" in others. In other words: love gives individuals "the benefit of the doubt" concerning issues that may arise. Love does not seek to find wrong where not wrong exists.
2. Rigid
"rejoices not in iniquity"
Even though love gives others "the benefit of the doubt" love does not condone sinful acts as OK. God's love is "tough love." Its standard of right is based upon what God's Word teaches and not what this sinful world allows as right. God's love is intolerant of willful sin and intentional wrongs.

3. Requiring
    "rejoices in the truth"
    The love of God requires that truth be upheld. There is "ABSOLUTE TRUTH." When questioned by Pilate as to whether or not He was "a king" Jesus answered: "You say rightly that I am a king. For this cause I was born, and <u>for this cause I have come into the world, that I should bear witness to the truth. Everyone who is of the truth hears My voice</u>" (John 18:37). In another place Jesus said: "<u>I am</u> the way, <u>the truth</u>, and the life. No man comes to the Father except by Me" (John 14:6). Jesus is The TRUTH. Love demands that we require "faith in Jesus Christ alone" for salvation. Any other belief is a lie and must be rejected.

III. v.. 7: **NATURE** of Love
    We see the nature of love in an individual by the standards that one holds dear to their heart. When God's love dominates one's life not only does that one hold high standards but lives by those standards.

A. ADVOCATE – "Bears All Things"
    To bear something means to take upon oneself a burden. As Christians there are many burdens which we take upon ourselves when we invited Jesus Christ into our lives as Lord. These three encompass all others:

1. Bears a Christlikeness of Order – Philippians 2:1-5
    Here we are commanded to "let this mind be in you which was also in Christ Jesus." In verses 1-4 we are given the qualities of one fulfilling this command.
    a. v. 1: Devotions
        (1). Consolation in Christ
        (2). Comfort of Love
        (3). Camaraderie of The Spirit = "fellowship"
        (4). Concern for The Brethren = "affection"
        (5). Compassion for The Lost = "mercy"
    b. v. 2: Disciplines
        (1). Participation = "fulfill"
        (2). Presentation = "being likeminded"

    (3). Passionate = "same love"
    (4). Peaceable = "one accord"
    (5). Purposeful = "one mind"
  c. v. 3-4: Deed Done = "be done"
    1. Honor Bound = "not through selfish ambition"
    2. Honest = "not … through conceit"
    3. Humble = "lowliness of mind"
    4. Honoring = "esteem others"
    5. Helpful = v. 4: "Let each of you look out not only for his own interests, but also for the interest of others."
    *. v. 5: Desired Outcome
       "Let this mind be in you which was in Christ Jesus."
2. Bears a Cross of Obedience – Luke 9:23
   To bear the cross that Jesus would give us to bear we must:
      a. Decide – "If anyone desires"
      b. Dedication – "to come after Me (Jesus)"
      c. Denial of Self – "let him deny himself"
      d. Daily Devotion – "take up his cross daily"
      e. Direction – "and follow me (Jesus)".
3. Bears a Concern for Others – Galatians 6:1-2
   It is the Christian's duty to watch over other Christians. Having observed another Christian overtaken in any tresspass the spiritual Christian is to offer a …
      1. Honoring Help
         "restore such a one in a spirit of gentleness"
      2. Humble Help
         "considering yourself lest you also be tempted"
      3. Honest Help
         "Bear one another's burdens"
      4. Heavenly Help
         "and so fulfill the law of Christ"

B. ASSUMPTION – "Believes All Things"

A right understanding of this phrase is important. This does not mean that love will believe any false teaching that comes along. The Christian's belief system is grounded because he is …
1. Convinced of The Word – 1 John 5:13
   a. Love Emmanuel
      "believe in the name of the Son of God"
   b. Life Eternal
      "know that we have eternal life"
   c. Live as Examples
      "continue to believe in the name of the Son of God"
2. Committed to The Word – 1 Corinthians 1:30 - 2:2
   a. Greatness of Christ – v. 30:
      "Christ Jesus who became for us …"
   b. Glory of Christ – 31:
      "He who glories, let him glory in the Lord"
   c. Gospel of Christ – v. 2
      "to know nothing … except Jesus Christ and Him crucified"
3. Confirmed by The Word – John 8:31-32

   To be confirmed by The Word on must "abide in The Word; the evidence of this abiding is that one …
   a. Lives The Word
      "you are Jesus' disciples indeed"
   b. Learns The Word
      "you shall know The Truth"
   c. Liberated by The Word
      "The Truth shall make you free"

C. ASSURANCE – "Hopes All Things"

The hope that we have in Christ Jesus gives us reasons to live in this life looking forward to the home that has been prepared for us in the after-life. This hope is seen in that the Christian can have …

1. Confidence to Stand – Hebrews 6:18-19
   a. Protected Character
      "we might have strong consolation, who have fled for refuge to lay hold of the hope set before us"
   b. Permanent Course
      "This hope we have as an anchor of the soul, both sure and steadfast"
   c. Presence of The Christ
      "the Presence behind the veil, where the forerunner has entered for us, even Jesus, having become High Priest forever according to the order of Melchizedek"
2. Clean Living to Shine Out – 1 John 3:2-3
   a. Expectation of Perfection
      "Beloved, now we are children of God; and it has not yet been revealed what we shall be, … but we shall be like Him"
   b. Example from the Pure
      "… when He is revealed …
         … we shall see Him as He is"
   c. Encouragement to Purity
      "And everyone who has this hope in Him purifies himself, just as He is pure"
3. Called to Testify of Salvation – 1 Peter 3:15-16
   a. Ready
      "But sanctify the Lord God in your hearts, and always be ready to give a defense"
   b. Representative
      "to everyone who asks you a reason for the hope that is in you, with meekness and fear"
   c. Reputation
      "having a good conscience, that when they defame you as evildoers, those who revile your good conduct in Christ may be ashamed"

D. ACCEPTANCE – "Endures All Things"
A Christian centered in the love of God will be able to endure many things; knowing that "if anyone suffers as a Christian, let him not be ashamed, but let him glorify God in this matter" (1 Peter 4:16). God is glorified when a Christian ...
1. Endure the Coaxing of The Wicked – James 1:12
   a. Temptation's Conquest
      "Blessed is the man who endures temptation"
   b. Triumph Conquering
      "for when he has been approved"
   c. Testimonial Crown
      "he will receive the crown of life"
   d. True Concern
      "which the Lord has promised to those who love Him"
2. Endure the Calamity in This World – 1 Peter 2:19-21
   a. v. 19: Conscience toward God
   b. v. 20: Commendable before God
   c. v. 21: Called of God
3. Endure the Chastening of Witness – Hebrews 12:7-11
   a. v. 7-10a: Personal Profit
   b. v. 10b: Partakers of God's Holiness
   c. v. 11: Peaceable Fruit of Righteousness
IV. v. 8-12: **NEVER-ENDING** Love

"Love never fails." Where everything else has fallen or cease to be we are guaranteed that "love will never fail." One of the reasons for this is the fact that: "God is love" (1 John 4:16). There are areas in this world that will fail even though mankind has placed much emphasis upon them. Before we look at some of these areas let us look at what we are taught in verse 10 which says: "when that which is perfect has come, then that which is in part will be done away." Just what is that "which is perfect"? Obviously, this reference cannot be speaking about Jesus Christ as some have taught being that it was penned after the ascension of our Lord. Nor can it be referring to the Church for the church had already been formed. However, the "Cannon of Scripture" was still being put together at the time of this writing. We accept that as the Bible was place together and then approved by the Church as the completed Word of God. Although for our purpose we do not have the space to give a detailed account: The 66 Books of the Bible is that "which is perfect." This being accepted then we can deal with the areas that will fail. These areas are …

A. SPIRITUAL SIGHT Fails

"Prophecies will fail" for we only "prophecy in part" (v. 8 & 9). The Old Testament prophets only prophesied what God gave them to share. Each prophecy was only a part of the story. No one prophet was able to give a full understanding of the prophesied event. We know that "God at various times and in various ways spoke in times past to the fathers by the prophets, has in these last days spoken to us by His Son" (Hebrews 1:1-2). The church and its doctrine has been "built on the foundation of the apostles and prophets, Jesus Christ Himself being the chief cornerstone" (Ephesians 2:20). The last apostle that we have was Paul for he said of himself: "that Jesus was seen by him last of all, as by one born out of due time, being the least of the apostles" (1 Corinthians 15:8-9). Since we now have the completed (perfect) Word of God there is no need for prophecy. Therefore prophecy has failed.

B. PHYSICAL PROFICIENCY Fails

"Where there are tongues, they will cease." "When I was a child, I spoke as a child, I understood as a child, I thought as a child; but when I became a man, I put away childish things." When the church was first being formed we find that men from at least seventeen different people groups had come to Jerusalem to worship. As the apostles spoke these different groups heard them speak in their own languages. This speaking in tongues was given that individual might come to know Jesus Christ as Savior and Lord. There were about three thousand souls added to the church that day (Acts 2). We are told that "tongues were for a sign to the unbelievers" (1 Corinthians 14:22). Tongues were given to the church body in its infancy (as a sign to the unbelievers that this new message was true) to help it grow. Now that the "perfect" = the completed Word of God – has come there is no need for the sign of tongues. "For when I was a child, I spoke as a child, I understood as a child, I thought as a child; but when I became a man, I put away childish thing" (v. 11). Those striving to hold on to "tongues" are refusing to grow up spiritually and remain in the spiritual childhood. It is time to put away "childish things and become a man." Therefore "tongues have ceased."

C. MENTAL MATURITY Fails

"Where there is knowledge, it will vanish away." "For now we see in a mirror dimly, but then face to face. Now I know in part, but then I shall know just as I also am known." There are many cases where the wisdom of man has vanished away to be known no more. One simple example is that we as a people can no longer make "real stained glass." The "stained glass" made today is only "colored glass." Real stained glass did not refract light as does the colored glass that we make today does. We are informed in 1 Corinthians 1:18-21, 26-29, & 31 that:

"For the message of the cross is foolishness to those who are perishing, but to us who are being saved it is the power of God.

For it is written: I will destrohy the wisdom of the wise, and bring to nothing the understanding of the prudent.

Where is the wise? Where is the scribe? Where is the disputer of this age? Has not God made foolish the wisdom of this world.

For since, in the wisdom of God, the world through wisdom did not know God, it pleased God through the foolishness of the message preached to save those who believe.

> For you see your calling, brethren, that not many wise according to the flesh, not many mighty, not many noble, are called.
> But God has chosen the foolish things of the world to put to shame the wise, and God has chosen the weak things of the world to put to shame the things which are mighty;
> and the base things of the world and the things which are despised God has chosen, and the things which are not, to bring to nothing the things that are.
> that no flesh should blory in His presence.
> that, as it is written, He who glories, let him glory in the Lord."

Therefore, the knowledge of this world has ceased to be effective and has vanished away. Any such knowledge that the world thinks that it finds also will vanish away before God and true wisdom.

V. v. 13: **NOBILITY** of Love
  A. GOOD – Salvation Given – "faith"
    * - Those Who Live By Faith

We must have faith, for "without faith it is impossible to please Him, for he who comes to God must believe that He is, and that He is a rewarder of those who diligently seek Him" (Hebrews 11:6). "For by grace you have been saved through faith, and that not of yourselves, it is the gift of God, not of works, lest anyone should boast. For we are God's workmanship, created in Christ Jesus for good works, which God prepared beforehand that we should walk in them" (Ephesians 2:8-10).

  B. GREAT – Security Guaranteed – "hope"
    * - Those Who Live In Hope

"For I consider that the sufferings of this present time are not worthy *to be compared* with the glory which shall be revealed in us. For the earnest expectation of the creation eagerly waits for the revealing of the sons of God. For the creation was subjected to futility, not willingly, but because of Him who subjected *it* in hope; because the creation itself also will be delivered from the bondage of corruption into the glorious liberty of the children of God. For we know that the whole creation groans and labors with birth pangs together until now. Not only *that,* but we also who have the firstfruits of the Spirit, even we ourselves groan within ourselves, eagerly waiting for the adoption, the redemption of our body. For we were saved in this hope, but hope that is seen is not hope; for why does one still hope for what he sees? But if we hope for what we do not see, we eagerly wait for *it* with perseverance" (Romans 8:18-25).

C. GREATEST – Sanctified Giving – "love"
   * - Those Who Live Through Love

As an aged Christian lay dying in Edinburgh, a friend called to say farewell. "I have just had three other visitors," said the dying man, "and with two of them I parted; but the third I shall keep with me forever." "Who are they?"

"The first was Faith, and I said, 'Goodbye, Faith! I thank God for your company ever since I first trusted Christ; but now I am going where faith is lost in sight.'

"Then came Hope. 'Farewell, Hope!' I cried. 'You have helped me in many an hour of battle and distress, but now I shall not need you, for I am going where hope passes into fruition.'

Last of all came Love. 'Love,' said I, 'you have indeed been my friend; you have linked me with God and with my fellow men; you have comforted and gladdened all my pilgrimage. But I cannot leave you behind; you must come with me through the gates, into the city of God, for love is perfected in heaven.' "
(1 Cor. 13) — *Sunday School Chronicle*
    Encyclopedia of 15,000 Illustrations: Signs of the Times.

XIX. v. 10:19-25: The Sanctuary (Congregational) Worship in The Lordship of Christ

<u>5. v. 24b: The Bolstering of Believers</u>
"Let us consider one another in order to stir up ... good works"

Since as Christians "we are His workmanship, created in Christ Jesus for good works, which God prepared beforehand that we should walk in them" (Ephesians 2:10) we are to have a character with is modeled after Jesus Christ. In Jesus' teaching that is referred to as "The Sermon on The Mount" we are given a description of The True Christian Character. This is a guide to how the followers of Jesus should live their lives in a world that rejects Him and us alike.

THE TRUE CHRISTIAN CHARACTER
Matthew 5:1-16

Intro. v. 1-2: Articulation of The How-To of

Jesus, having gone up into a mountain followed by "the multitudes", sat down and began to teach. Some have compared the New Testament "Beattitudes" of "The Sermon on the Mount" to the Old Testament "Ten Commandment." Thus, what the Ten Commandments was for the nation of Israel the Beattitudes are for Christians.

A. Blessings – "His Disciples"

If one desires to be blessed that one must be willing to become a follower of Christ. There is a cost to becoming a disciple of Jesus. As Jesus mentioned: "If the world hates you, you know that it hated Me before it hated you" (John 15:18).

B. Beliefs – "came to Him"

To have a right belief system one must "learn of Me" (Matthew 11:29) Jesus enlightens us.

C. Betterments – "He ... taught them"

Jesus' teachings were designed to help individuals better themselves in this life. Remember, Jesus is the creator of all life and as such knows what we need to have the best life possible.

The Attitudes that a Christian should have in completing the kingdom work of Christ are …

I. v. 3: Appalled by our Humanness
- "the poor in spirit"

When we look at ourselves and look at mankind in general we should be revolted by what we see. Jesus, when referring to mankind, said that there was no one that was good, no not one. When God "looked down from heaven upon the children of men, to see if there were any that did understand, and see Him. They are all gone aside, they are all together become filthy: there is none that doeth good, no, not one." (Psalm 14:2-3). The idea that mankind is somehow basically good is a false belief promoted by the devil to side track people from seeking a Savior, which everyone needs.

* - Pardoned in our Confession – LOVE
- "for theirs is the kingdom of God"

When one recognizes their personal wickedness that individual begins the journey to accept the forgiveness of sin offered by Christ based on His shed blood on the cross of Calvary. This forgiveness produces the first fruit of the Spirit which is LOVE. As one is surrounded by the love of God found in Christ that love begins to become a part of that individual that can be seen by others and shared with others. This is the necessary first step for anyone whom desires to become a disciple of Christ and to have a right relationship with God.

II. v. 4: Anguish of the Heart
- "they that mourn"

When we understand the terrible condition of the human soul, because we are cursed with sin, it creates a mournful spirit within. We understand that "without Christ we can do nothing" and that in truth "without Christ we are nothing" therefore we are grieved in our hearts and in our spirits. Even after one has accepted Jesus Christ as their Savior and Lord that individual can still sin and grieve God and in turn grieve their-self. Paul said that when he did "that which he would not" (sin) it would grieve his soul. In other words, when we fall into a sinful act we should mourn within ourselves and desire to be cleansed.

* - Present from the Comforter – JOY

Jesus informed us that the Holy Spirit is "The Comforter." Therefore we must acknowledge that it is the presence and control of the Holy Spirit in our lives which brings us comfort. Jesus also informed us that it was the Holy Spirit's job to convict the world of sin. When we are convicted of our "falling short of the glory of God" and we repent of that sin then the Holy Spirit can bring comfort into our lives. This comfort leads to the second fruit of the Spirit – Joy. To have real joy in one's life an individual must yield to the conviction of the Holy Spirit and come to Christ for forgiveness of sin and to be cleansed from all unrighteousness.

III. v. 5: Attitude of Humility

- "the meek"

The term "meek" has been one that has been hard to define in today's culture. "Meekness" has the idea of understanding that without Christ in our lives "we can do nothing." It also understands that without Christ in our lives "we are nothing." Today's culture is hard pressed to accept these ideas. It has been popularized that there is "good in everyone if you just look for it." This popular idea is contrary with the teaching of Scripture. The Bible (God's Word) makes it plan that mankind's best efforts at morality is as "filthy rags" before a Holy God. Meekness understands that we can accomplish nothing by ourselves. We must have God's intervention in our lives if we are to meet His standards of righteousness.

* - Prominence of Consequence – PEACE

- "they shall inherit the earth"

Someone with a "meek spirit" will understand that there are consequences attached to every action. An individual may be able to decide what actions they are going to commit: That same individual will not be able to determine the consequences of those actions. God's Word informs us of a spiritual law which is: What you sow (actions you commit), you shall reap (consequences of those actions). No one can separate the results from the actions. The "meek" individual can have the third fruit of the Spirit – Peace – because they sow actions that have determined righteous results. This individual is at peace with God and man because they have lived a true "meek" life.

IV. v. 6: Appetite that is Healthy
- "hunger and thirst after righteousness"

Much has been written, spoken, and presented about eating the right kinds of food so that they body will be healthy. This same idea can be applied to the spiritual life as well. We are instructed throughout Scripture to read, study, meditate, and memorize the Word of God. A Christian should have a healthy appetite for the Scriptures. Partaking of a proper menu of Scripture will help a Christian have a healthy spiritual life in the same way that a proper diet of food will help one to have a healthy body. God's Word should be taken into one's life with the understanding that it is our spiritual nourishment and it is necessary for our continued spiritual health.

* - Partakers of Contentment – LONGSUFFERING
- "they shall be filled"

As a Christian partakes of God's Word in a regular proper procedure of study, devotion, and memorization that individual will then be "filled" or satisfied. Spiritual satisfaction will lead to one having a sense of "contentment." Scripture says that "godliness with contentment is great gain." When a Christian has reached a point of contentment with God and spiritual things that individual then can have the fourth fruit of the Spirit which is patience. An individual is willing to "wait on the Lord" when they have reached a point of spiritual satisfaction. This patience allows us to "wait"

on the Lord's timetable and not to expect things to happen according to our own personal agenda.
V. v. 7: Accept the Helpless
- "the merciful"

As Disciples of Christ we are commanded to follow Jesus' example. Then over and over again we are told about the compassion of Christ. As we live a life based upon Christ's example we should begin to share in the compassion of Christ for others. This compassion will lead us to be "merciful" toward others. We will begin to show a concern for others based on the concern that God has for all. We will begin to see others through the eyes of Christ.

* - Passionate Care – GENTLENESS
- "they shall obtain mercy"

The most misquoted verse in the Bible today gives understanding to this passage of Scripture. Jesus did say: "Judge not that ye be not judged." However that is not where Jesus' statement ended. Jesus continued when He said: "For with the measure of judgment that ye judge with, you yourself will be judged by." In other words Jesus did not say that we could not judge others or their situations: What Jesus said was that when you do judge others and their situations the <u>standards that you use to judge others will be applied to yourself when others judge you.</u> When an individual truly understands this Biblical concept they will learn to be gentle when dealing with other people.

VI. v. 8: Awareness of the Holy
- "pure in heart"

One whom has actually been born anew by the blood of the cross of Christ will have an appreciation of the perfectness of Christ and everything that is Godly. We are told that Christ was "tempted in all manner like we are, yet without sin." And then we are commanded to be "Christ-Like." We, as Christians, have been command to strive to live the "perfect life" without sin. Because we still have the old nature (old man) within us fighting against the new nature (new man) we will at times yield to temptation and commit "acts" of sin. Even so, we are to have hearts that are pure. Our lives should always be characterized by a longing to do that which is pure in the sight of God. When we do sin it should grieve us, and it will if our hearts are pure.

* - Presence of The Creator – GOODNESS
  - "they shall see God"

An individual that lives a life based upon the standards of God in Christ Jesus will be able to "see God" active in their life. As the presence of God becomes more real an individual will be able to live out the goodness that will please our heavenly Father. This sixth fruit of the Spirit become the general character of one in whom has become fully away of the holiness of God and is striving to be Christ-Like in every way.

VII. v. 9: Application of the Helpful
  - "the peacemakers"

A "peacemaker" is one that strives to bring individuals to a right relationship with God through Jesus Christ. For an individual to have real peace that one must first have peace with their creator – Yahweh = The God of the Bible. This primary peace will lead to having peace with one's self and having peace with others. After one has receive this peace by accepting forgiveness of sin through the shed blood of Christ then one can begin to share this peace with other. This is one of the greatest works that anyone could take upon themselves to do. This work of "peacemaking" is called by most by another name: "Soul-winning." When one makes this their main focus of life they will be …

* - Presented as the Children – FAITH
  - "shall be called the children of God"

The greatest witness that one has that they are the children of God is the passion that they have about sharing the plan of salvation found only in Jesus Christ. If we truly believe that there is only one way of salvation then we should be all means be sharing it with everyone that we can. We will not let anything keep us from putting forth this message to the world. The Christian message of salvation is not the best thing going, IT IS THE **ONLY** THING GOING. The Christian Faith is a exclusive belief system. Jesus said: "No one comes to the Father but by Me." There is no salvation in any other and there is only one name that will form a right relationship with God and that name is Jesus Christ. If one confidently believes this then there is no alternative but to share this message with as many as possible. As this passion is seen by others they will recognize the individual with it as "a child of God." As we live out this passion the seventh fruit of the Spirit begins to grow in us and that is FAITH. As we share the gospel message and see others come to faith in Christ our own faith will grow.

VIII. v. 10: Aqueous to the Harmful
- "persecuted for righteousness's sake"

As a Christian lives for Christ in this lost world there will be times when we are persecuted for our faith in Christ. Jesus said that the world hated Him and that it would also hate us. We understand that there will be those whom desire to hurt us because of our stand for the Christian faith. We as Christ's followers accept this as just a simple fact of life. We realize that when persecution comes our ways that it is just a normal part of being a Christian.

* - Participation in the Church – MEEKNESS
- "there is the kingdom of heaven"

As the Christian accepts the fact that we will be persecuted for our faith in Jesus Christ we learn to receive it with a "meek and mild spirit." The reason that I conclude that this also means participating in the Church is because we are commanded to assemble together and to build up "the body of Christ" = The Church. By working through the Church (Christ's body) we have the opportunity to share in "the kingdom of heaven" here on earth. Jesus gave us the example of attending the synagogue (Church) on a regular basis. Then He said that He came to build the Church. After the resurrection of Christ we see the Church founded and growing throughout the world. Then in Hebrews we are commanded "not to forsake the assembling of ourselves together, as the manner of some is." It becomes obvious that we as Christians are to participate in the fellowship of the "body of Christ" which is the local Church assembly. As we do this we begin to show the eighth fruit of the Spirit which is meekness. This meekness is an understanding that we cannot live the Christian life in isolation; we need others to help us stay faithful and to grow in our Christian life.

IX. v. 11: Acceptance of Heartache
- "when men shall revile you, and persecute you, and shall say all manner of evil against you falsely."

This is closely related to the last quality of knowing that we will suffer some harm for being a Christian. This deals more with the personal attacks that one will receive because of our faith in Christ. We will endure persecution for our faith in general, but we will also have to accept <u>personal</u> attacks that others direct at us. We can deal with these personal attacks when we understand that the attacks are not really against us but that we are in a spiritual battle. In Ephesians we are told that we are fighting not against flesh and blood but against principalities, powers, and rulers of darkness. Understanding this we realize that the attacks are really the spiritual darts of the devil aimed at us to sidetrack us from the real work of the gospel.

* - Point of Conflict – SELF-CONTROL
- "for my {Christ} sake"

When we understand that these attacks are spiritual attacks and not really personal attacks we can display the ninth fruit of the Spirit which is self-control. We will not feel the necessity of attacking back or defending ourselves. We will focus on answering the spiritual needs of others and not dealing in personalities. We will be able to control the temptation of focusing upon ourselves instead of upon the real needs. The Holy Spirit will help us control our tongues and our actions when dealing with other. Then we will be able to give Christ the glory and not yield to the wiles of the devil.

X. v. 12: Award of Honor

- "Rejoice, and be exceeding glad: ... for so persecuted they the prophets which were before you."

Christ knew what we would face because of our faith. He also provided three encouragements that will help us endure anything that this world throws at us:

(1). Ecstatic Joy

We can rejoice in the Lord always. Our joy comes not from circumstances, but our joy come from a relationship with a loving heavenly Father. So no matter what we experience we can find fantastic joy in the Lord.

(2). Exceeding Gladness

We are also given a spirit of gladness. We are given many reasons to be glad and not sad. God, through Christ, has given us many reason to be happy. The results of a life lives in Christ for God bring many blessings and many glad tidings.

(3). Example to Follow

We can be encouraged when we realize that we are not the first to be persecuted for our faith. There have been many that have given us examples to follow as we live for Christ. Many of those examples are found in Scripture. But many more are found in the historical studies of the Church. We find many individuals who suffered much for

Christ. We can be encouraged that no matter what we go through we will be able to endure just like our predecessors in the faith of Christ.

* - Promise of Christ – AGAINST SUCH THERE IS NO LAW
 - "for great is your reward in heaven"

The greatest reward that a child of God can receive will be when we get to heaven and stand before Christ at the judgment seat of Christ and have Him declare to us: "Well done thou good and faithful servant, enter ye into the rest of your Lord." What better thing could we ever receive for a life lived for Christ?

@. v. 13-16: Applying of the Principles

We have been called to share these principles with the world. We can do this by being the "salt and the light of the world." When we do these we act as ...

1. v. 13a: Preserver
    - "you are the salt of the earth"

    Salt was primarily used as a preservative in the Biblical days. Since they did not have refrigerants they had to use salt. Today we as Christians are to live in such a way as to preserve the faith of Christ in this society. We are to help safeguard the morality in our culture. Because of our presence the godly standards should be preserved.

2. v. 13b: Protector
    - "to be thrown out and trampled underfoot by men"

    Salt that has lost its use for the table is used in a way the beings protection to the people that use it. For example, we prepare the roadways for safe journey by placing salt upon them to protect from ice during bad weather. Christians should act as protectors of their surroundings by being a barrier against the acceptance of sinful actions. The Christian's teachings and lifestyles should point to the way of right. What a nation sows, that it will also reap. Christian salt should help less sin to be sowed and therefore help reap a better harvest of consequences.

3. v. 14a: Prominence
    - "You are the light of the world"

    The Christian should live in such a way that the world sees the good light of example lives out. The message that we have is the only true light that shines on the way of salvation that leads to a right relationship with God. We must shine bright in this world of darkness.
4. v. 14b: Presence
    - "a city that is set on a hill cannot be hidden"

    The Christian light should be lived in such a way that it cannot be hidden by the sinful nature of our world. Just as a city set upon a hill cannot be hid so our Christian lives should be seen by the world no matter what circumstances may arise.
5. v. 15: Purpose
    - "it gives light to all who are in the house"

    When a person turns on a light they do so to illuminate the area for everyone that is in that location. Just so, we as Christians are to shine forth our Christian influence that everyone that meets us will know whom we live for – Christ. Anyone that sees us should comprehend that we belong to Christ because of our witness.
6. v. 16a: Presentation
    - "Let you light so shine before men"

    The witness that Christians are to give is based in the good works that they do. Jesus made the point that it is not enough to say that you love someone without showing that you love them by your actions. James makes the point that if your faith does not produce good works then you have a false faith. Paul makes the point that we are saved by grace, but we are saved by a grace that produces the good works that God has foreordained that we are to do. Our good works are the witness that the lost world can see giving evidence that we belong to Christ.

7. v. 16b: Point to God
    - "that they may see your good works
      and glorify your Father in heaven."
    We are commanded that "if someone is to receive glory, let him glory only in the cross of Christ." Everything that we do or say we are to do or say in the name of Jesus Christ that the Father in heaven may be glorified. We must let the world know that we are not doing good because we are such good people or that the ones that we are helping deserve the help, but we are to inform the world that what we are doing comes out of a relationship with the God of the Bible – Yahweh, and that this relationship is formed through faith in Jesus Christ. It is because of this relationship that we do the good works that we do and we do all things for His glory alone.

Let us do our best to allow this true Christian character to be seen in our lives as we strive to live for Jesus Christ our Savior and Lord and to give glory to our heavenly Father.

XIX. v. 10:19-25: The Sanctuary (Congregational) Worship in The Lordship of Christ
6. v. 25a: The Brotherhood of Believers
"not forsaking the assembling of ourselves together, as the manner of some"

Now a People
1 Peter 2:4-12

I. v. 4-8: Dividing Beliefs Listed

Before we discuss the special qualities of the People of God we are going to look at the beliefs that make us as Christians different from those that are not part of the family of God.

  A. v. 4-5: Purpose of Spirituality

In our world today most people are "spiritually" minded. You see people interest in the "spiritual things" in what they watch on TV, read, and discuss in public forums. But this type of "spirituality" is not what the Bible refers to as "spiritual." The difference is seen in the relationship that individual have with God (the God of the Bible).

    1. World – Shuns God's Gift

The world has chosen to reject the plan of salvation that God has prepared. Those that claim to be spiritual but refuse to come to God on His terms will miss God. God is so far above us that we are not capable of coming to Him on our terms. We must seek God based on the way that He has designed. The worldly mind rejects the cornerstone of God's plan—Jesus Christ.

    2. Believers – Sacrifice to God's Glory

When one comes to God by His plan that individual will give as a sacrifice to God His own life. We are encouraged in Romans 12:1: "I beseech you therefore, brethren, by the mercies of God, that you present your bodies a

living sacrifice, holy, actable to God, which is your reasonable service." People who are truly spiritual will make this sacrifice that God has asked for.
- B. v. 6-7a: Preciousness of The Savior
  1. World – Confounded
      The lost world is at a loss to explain Jesus. In the first chapter of John we are told that Jesus "came unto His own, and His own received Him not." We are also told that He "came into the world and the world <u>knew Him not</u>." This is why the world in general is confused about Jesus and have problem understanding His followers.
  2. Believers – Confesses
      Christians confess that Jesus is the "cornerstone" of our lives. He is the reason for our existence. He is the purpose of our lives. Jesus Christ is our all. Christ is precious to us in all things.
- C. v. 7b-8: Presented Salvation
  1. World – v. 7b & 8: Salvation is Cast Away Lightly
      The world ignores, very flippantly, the forgiveness that is offered in Jesus Christ. They do not understand the necessity of accepting Christ if they are to have a relationship with the God of the universe. They live life as if there were no eternity to be dealt with.
  2. Believers – v. 7c: Salvation is the Cornerstone of Life
      The real child of God, whom has been adopted in Jesus Christ, will make the Christian experience the most important thing in their life. For we understand, as Christ taught, that if a man was to gain the whole world yet lose his soul he will have lost everything.

II. v. 9-10: Designation of Believers' Longings

As Christians we have been made into something new in Christ; "for anyone in Christ is a new creature, old things have passed away, behold all things have become new." This newness is expressed in that we are a ...

1. Picked People – "a chosen generation"

   Christ has chosen us to be his people. Christ has invited us to be a part of what He is doing in the world. When we accept His invitation we then are chosen to be "His People."

2. Priestly People – "a royal priesthood"

   Christians have been chosen to be the priest of Christ. A priest had two functions: The first function was to represent the people to God. We do this by praying for the people involved in our lives. We present to God the needs of those around us and represent them to our God. The second function of a priest was to represent God to the people. We do this when we share the gospel message of Jesus Christ with the lost and dying world. We also do this by "teaching them to observe all the commandments that Jesus taught us." We are the priests of Christ.

3. Pure People – "a holy nation"

   We have been given the command to be like Christ: Hence the name "Christian." The word "holy" means to be "separate." Our standards of life are to be such that make us a people that are different from the world. What we consider to be right or wrong is based upon the standards of God as revealed in the Bible and not those of the worlds corrupted points of view.

4. Peculiar People

   Because we live by standards (those of The Bible) that the world cannot understand we should seem as "peculiar" to the world. We should not fit in with the world and the way that it does things. The lost world should perceive in us a difference that marks us as not

of this world. Thus they will wonder "what is *wrong* with us" and we will tell them what is *right* with us.
5. Praising People

As children of God we should be proclaiming the praises of Jesus because He has brought us out of darkness into His marvelous light. We have been given many reasons to sing and shout the glory of Christ. We must let the world know of the love and honor that we have for Jesus Christ. We have been appointed His witnesses in this world.

6. Pointed People – "a called people"

Christ has given us a specific call (or job to do). We have been given direction as to what God would have us to do in this world during the time that He chooses to leave us here. Jesus said that He came to "seek and to save that which was lost." He then said: "that as the Father had sent Him, even so send I you." We have been given the call to "seek and to save that which is lost in this world." We can do this by fulfilling THE GREAT COMMISSION as found in Matthew 28:18-20. Let us be obedient to the will of God in completing the task that He has called us to do.

7. Providential People – "people of God"

This is our greatest calling: We have been called to be the PEOPLE OF GOD. We must take great care in that everything that we do or say is done in ways that will properly represent Him to the world. When others look at us, we may be "the only Jesus that they have ever seen." We must life as Christ would have us live and not according to our own personal agendas. We are to be known as the people of God.

III. v. 11-12: Dearly Beloved Lived-Out

When we have become the people of God we should strive to live out our faith. A faith that is lived our will have these qualities.

1. Passionate People – "dearly beloved"

We live our lives for Jesus Christ because He first loved us. We are told that Christ died for us while we

were still sinners. God loved us enough to "bankrupt" heaven that our salvation could be purchased. We are loved by God and this love motivates us to become obedient children.
2. Passers-By – "strangers" in this world

    We can live by the standards of God and not by the standards of this world because we do not belong to this world. This world is not our home. Because the world first hated Jesus it will also hate us. Because we know this we are not offended when the world rejects our message of salvation found in Christ. We are not discouraged because of suffering for Christ but encouraged in that we are suffering because we are being obedient to our Savior.
3. Place Oriented – (looking for a city) – pilgrims

    In the book of Hebrews we are told that Abraham was "a pilgrim that was looking for a city that was not made with hands, but a heavenly city." We as Christians also are looking for that city of God that one day we will be going to. Jesus told us: "that He was going to prepare for us a place, and that if He was preparing a place for us, that one day He would come again and receive us to Himself that where He dwells we also could dwell." Our focus is not upon the things of this world but upon eternal things.
4. Pure Persuasion – "abstain from lusts"

    We, as Christ's followers, understand that we must reject the temptations of this world. We know that they are designed to take our focus off of Christ and to sidetrack the lives that we are living for Christ. We, as newborn children of God in Christ, are not perfect yet we are striving to become more Christ-like each day. Therefore we resist the devil and have the promise that he will flee, for a time, from us.
5. Providential Priorities – "honest lifestyle"

    Jesus told us that "if we love Him we will keep His commandments." Jesus also told us that the "world would know that we are His disciples in that we keep

His commandments." We express our faith when we place the will of God above our own wills. We understand that God knows all things, including the future, and therefore His will is the best things for us even when we cannot comprehend that truth.
6. Performance Seen – "good works"

As we express our faith by doing good works we are doing so that "the world can see our good works which cannot be hid (like a city set upon a hill) that in seeing our good works our heavenly Father will be glorified." The good that we do is done in the name of Jesus Christ and to show that He has made a difference in our own lives and can make a difference in the lives of those whom we are sharing with.
7. Purpose Driven Life – "glorify God"

Jesus said that it was His purpose to "glorify God." Jesus died on the cross of Calvary to accomplish His purpose. We do not know what it will cost us personally to "glorify God", but whatever it is we are willing to pay. When one lives out the faith of Jesus Christ to glorify God it becomes the number one purpose of our lives. Any other purpose comes second to this one. If this is not the number one purpose of one's life then Christ is not "Lord" of that life.

*. Dedication Bolstered by Love

If one has believed and accepted Christ as Savior, has developed the believer's longings, and is living out their faith in Christ then these evidences will be seen in that person's relationship with the church:

A. Eternal Focus

We understand that the Church is Christ's institution and not an institution of man's creation. The Church body will go into eternity and will last forever as the body of Christ. Because of this our personal focus will be on eternal things. We understand that the things of earth will fade away and not last, but the things of God

will last forever. We will focus our energies upon these eternal things.
B. Everlasting Family
We will understand that the Church is our real family. The old saying: that blood is thicker than water may be true; but it is also true that spirit is thicker than blood. Our Church family is one that will last into eternity and not end when we leave this earth. As individuals are born into the family of God, they become heirs and joint-heirs with Christ of eternal things. We all become brothers and sisters in Christ for all eternity.
C. Encouraging Friends
One of the greatest things about the Church family is that they are also encouraging friends. We develop friendships that will last for all eternity. We encourage one another in an unfriendly world. We have a place to come for protection and support when we have been down-trodden by the world.
*. Energetically Faithful
Because of all the benefits of being part of the Church we should put all our efforts into being faithful to it and its functions. Remember The Church is Jesus' Church.

XIX. v. 10:19-25: The Sanctuary (Congregational) Worship in The Lordship of Christ

<u>7. v. 25b: The Building-Up of Believers</u>
"but exhorting one another,
and so much the more as you see the Day approaching."

Comfort Through Suffering
2 Corinthians 1:3-11

Intro. Word Study: Exhortation
We are encouraged to "exhort one another" as we are journeying through this life. What does this mean?

A. Exhortation = παράκλησις = paraklēsis
In this case it gives great help to us in understanding what the phrase means when we look at the Greek word that is used.

B. Paraklesis = "Comfort"
The base meaning of the word "paraklesis" means "comfort." Jesus tells us that when the "Comforter {The Holy Spirit} comes … He will glorify Me, for He will take of what is Mine and declare it to you" (John 16:13-14). We know that the Holy Spirit is the Comforter because the Greek word for Holy Spirit is "paraklet."

C. Comfort is Gained Through Suffering
When someone is going through a time of crises that one will do one of two things: They will either push away the Holy Spirit {God} or refuse to receive comfort or they will pull closer to the Holy Spirit {God} and find the true …

1. v. 3: Source of All Comfort = God
"Blessed be the God and Father of our Lord Jesus Christ, the Father of mercies and God of all comfort."
Since the Holy Spirit {God} is the source of comfort the only way individuals will find true comfort is to release themselves to God. The comfort that God gives us is through Jesus Christ as taught in 2 Thessalonians 2:16-17 which says: "Now may our Lord Jesus Christ Himself, and our God and Father, who has loved us and

given *us* everlasting consolation and good hope by grace, comfort your hearts and establish you in every good word and work." The
- a. Basis of our Comfort is our Hope by Grace
- b. Belief of our Comfort is in our Hearts as a Gift
- c. Building of our Comfort is seen our Good words and work.

2. v. 4: Sharing of Comfort

"who comforts us in all our tribulation, that we may be able to comfort those who are in any trouble, with the comfort with which we ourselves are comforted by God."

God comforts us in our troubles so that we will be able to comfort others during their times of trouble. We are to share this comfort "that their hearts may be encouraged (comforted), being knit together in love, and *attaining* to all riches of the full assurance of understanding, to the knowledge of the mystery of God, both of the Father and of Christ" (Colossians 2:2). Our sharing of God's comfort will produce three results in others:
- a. Knit Together in Love
  There will be a bond formed that is uniquely Christian. We are "one in the bond of love."
- b. Kinship of Understanding
  This sharing will help fellow brothers and sisters in Christ be confident (assured) of their personal faith in Jesus Christ.
- c. Knowledge of the Mystery of God
  This sharing will help the family of God learn more about how God works with us through our Lord and Savior Jesus Christ.

3. v. 5: Savior of Comfort

"For as the sufferings of Christ abound in us, so our consolation also abounds through Christ."

"Beloved, do not think it strange concerning the fiery trial which is to try you, as though some strange thing happened to you; but rejoice to the extent that you partake of Christ's sufferings, that when His glory is revealed, you may also be glad with exceeding joy. If you are reproached for the name of Christ, blessed *are you,* for the Spirit of glory and of God rests upon you. On their part He is blasphemed, but on your part He is glorified. … Yet if *anyone suffers* as a Christian, let him not be ashamed, but let him glorify God in this matter" (1 Peter 4:12-16). We are willing to be comforted while partaking of Christ's sufferings because of our …

    a. Belief Concerning This Suffering
        → It is common and proof of our faith
    b. Bonus Received Through Suffering
        → We will be Rewarded = See Matthew 5:11-12
    c. Blessing Given Through Suffering
        → Christ will be glorified in us

4. v. 6: Seen Witness of Comfort

"Now if we are afflicted, it is for your consolation and salvation, which is effective for enduring the same sufferings which we also suffer. Or if we are comforted, it is for your consolation and salvation."

We have many examples from Christ down to modern times of individuals whom have suffered affliction and then where comforted. Paul said that the things his suffered and the comfort that he had received was to promote salvation in others. From this we learn that we are to be …

    a. Witnesses of Trials – "afflicted"
    b. Warmers of Hearts – "your consolation"
    c. Winners of Souls – "and salvation"

5. v. 7: Steadfastness Built Through Comfort

"And our hope for you is steadfast, because we know that as you are partakers of the sufferings, so also you will partake of the consolation."

"The Spirit Himself bears witness with our spirit that we are children of God, and if children, then heirs-- heirs of God and joint heirs with Christ, if indeed we suffer with *Him,* that we may also be glorified together" (Romans 8:16-17). Because we suffer with Christ we partake in His comfort in that we are ...

    a. Involved with God – "we are children of God"
    b. Inheritance with Christ – "joint heirs with Christ"
    c. Intensity in Christ – "glorified together"

6. v. 8-10: Sureness (Trust) Through Comfort
   a. v. 8: Knowledge

"For we do not want you to be ignorant, brethren, of our trouble which came to us in Asia: that we were burdened beyond measure, above strength, so that we despaired even of life."

We recognize that suffering is a part of life. "Man *that is* born of a woman *is* of few days, and full of trouble" (Job 14:1). Accepting this will keep one from becoming bitter about life in general.

   b. v. 9: Kinship

"Yes, we had the sentence of death in ourselves, that we should not trust in ourselves but in God who raises the dead."

We recognize that "it is appointed for men to die once, but after this the judgment" (Hebrews 9:27). Death is a part of life because all mankind have the curse of Adam upon them [the curse of sin = "The wages of sin is death" (Romans 3:23).] Therefore "let us hear the conclusion of the whole matter: Fear God and keep His commandment, for this is man's all. For God will bring every work into judgment, including every secret thing, whether good or evil" (Ecclesiastes 12:13-14).

    c. v. 10: King of kings
       "who delivered us from so great a death, and does deliver us; in whom we trust that He will still deliver us."
       Hence we are to Trust the Lord for our every need in good times and bad times. We are taught in the Proverbs the results when we "Trust in the Lord with all our hearts" (Proverbs 3:5-6).
        (1). v. 5b: Release Ourselves to God
           "lean not unto thine own understanding"
        (2). v. 6a: Remind Others of God
           "In all thy ways acknowledge Him"
             [Colossian 3:17: "Whatsoever ye do in word or deed, do all in the name of the Lord Jesus, giving thanks to God and the Father by Him."]
        (3). v. 6b: Roadway to Follow in God
           "and He shall direct thy paths"
             [Psalm 119:105: "Thy word is a lamp unto my feet, and a light unto my path."]

7. v. 11: Schooled by Suffering into Comfort
   "you also helping together in prayer for us, that thanks may be given by many persons on our behalf for the gift granted to us through many."
   As we experience suffering and trials in our lives we should ask God what He would desire to teach us during this time of conflict. Paul said that the Corinthians had learned three things through sharing in the sufferings he had endured for their sake. They learned …
    a. The Call of Prayer – "prayer for us"
    b. A Concern by many People – "thanks given by many persons on our behalf"
    c. Caring Present shared – "gift granted to us"

*. Text: Swelling (increase) of Comfort

"and so much the more as you see the Day approaching."

As we consider the day of the Lord's coming is getting nearer and nearer we are commanded to give encouragement more and more. This would encourage the Church body to meet more regularly and fellowship more often. As "we, according to his promise, look for new heavens and a new earth, wherein dwells righteousness. Beloved, seeing that ye look for such things, be diligent that ye may be found of Him in peace, without spot, and blameless" (2 Peter 3:13-14). So as we give one another comfort we are to do so being ...

a. Peaceable – "peace"

"Be of the same mind toward one another: do not set your mind on high things, but associate with the humble. Do not be wise in your own opinion. Repay no one evil for evil. Have regard for good things in the sight of all men. If it is possible, as much as depends on you, live peaceably with all men" (Romans 12:16-18).

b. Pure – "without spot"

"Seeing ye have purified your souls in obeying the truth through the Spirit unto unfeigned love of the brethren, *see that ye* love one another with a pure heart fervently" (1 Peter 1:22).

c. Presentable – "blameless"

"For it is God which works in you both to will and to do of *his* good pleasure. Do all things without murmurings and disputings: That ye may be blameless and harmless, the sons of God, without rebuke, in the midst of a crooked and perverse nation, among whom ye shine as lights in the world; Holding forth the word of life" (Philippians 2:13-16).

**XX. v. 10:26-39: The Training of
The Lordship of Christ**
A. v. 26-31: Representation of the Future
 1. v. 26-27: Warning of Judgment
   a. Preaching of the Right Gospel
   b. Persistent Refusal of the Gift
   c. Predictable Repercussion of Guilt – v. 27
 2. v. 28-29: Witnesses of Judgment
   a. Sentence of Guilt – based upon the Law
   b. Son of God Trampled Underfoot
   c. Spirit of Grace Insulted
 3. v. 30-31: Working of Judgment
   a. Father's Right = "Vengeance is Mine"
   b. Future Judgment by the Son {"The LORD"}
   c. "Fearful Thing to fall into the hands of the living God"
B. v. 32-34: Receiving of Faith
 1. Struggles with Sufferings
   a. Illumination
   b. Inclusion – "endured"
   c. Intensity – "great struggle with sufferings"
 2. Spectacles of Scorn
   a. Accusations – "reproaches"
   b. Anguish – "Tribulations"
   c. Associations – "became companions of those who were so treated"
 3. Sharing of the Splendid
   a. Empathetic Personality – "compassion on me"
   b. Endure the Plundering of our goods
   c. Enduring Possession … in heaven
C. v. 35-39: Reward of the Faithful
 1. v. 35: Promises of God
   a. Principles of – "therefore"
   b. Preserved – "cast not away"
   c. Prize – "which has great reward"
 2. v. 36-37: Pattern of Good
   a. Practice of Faith –"after ye have done the will of God"
   b. Promise – "receive the promise

  c. Preview – v. 37: "For yet a little while, and He who is coming will come and will not tarry."
 3. v. 38-39: Permanence Guaranteed
  a. Perception in the Savior – "live by faith"
  b. Pleasure of the Sovereign – "not drawback"
  c. Permanence of the Soul – v. 39: "But we are not of those who draw back to perdition, but of those who believe to the saving of the soul."

****

XX. v. 10:26-39: The Training of
       The Lordship of Christ
 A. v. 26-31: Representation of the Future
  1. v. 26-27: Warning of Judgment
  a. Preaching of the Right Gospel
   "received the knowledge of the truth"
  Jesus said "for this cause I have come into the world, that I should bear witness to the truth" (John 18:37). "Jesus is the way, the truth, and the life. No one comes to the Father except through Him" (John 14:6). "For this is good and acceptable in the sight of God our Savior, who desires all men to be saved and to come to the knowledge of the truth" (1 Timothy 2:3-4).
  b. Persistent Refusal of the Gift
   "if we sin willfully after we have received the knowledge … there no longer remains a sacrifice for sins"
  The Jews as a nation had received the knowledge of the true Messiah. Here they are informed that if they reject this knowledge there is no other "sacrifice for sins." {Note: This is not speaking about someone who has accepted Jesus as Savior: Rather it is speaking about someone who has understanding about whom Jesus is and refuses to accept Him in the free pardon of sin that He offers.}

c. Predictable Repercussion of Guilt – v. 27
Those whom reject the Messiah know that there is a eternal punishment that is forthcoming = "and anyone not found written in the Book of Life was cast into the lake of fire" (Revelation 20:15).
2. v. 28-29: Witnesses of Judgment
Here the punishment of rejection of grace is compared with the rejection of obedience to the Law
a. Sentence of Guilt – based upon the Law
It was common knowledge to the Jew that if someone was accused of breaking the Law of Moses that two or three witnesses were required for proof. If the criminal had committed a crime punishable by death the sentence was carried forth without mercy.
b. Son of God Trampled Underfoot
Since the Law of Moses was carried out with such force the question is put us as to "how much worse punishment do you suppose will one be though worthy who" rejects the only begotten Son of God and the sacrifice that He made upon the cross of Calvary. To reject Jesus is to reject the plan of salvation that God Himself has put into place and to compare it to a common place thing of no value.
c. Spirit of Grace Insulted
Also, to reject Jesus is to insult the Holy Spirit because "He has come to convict the world of sin, and of righteousness, and of judgment: of sin, because they do not believe in Jesus; of righteousness, because Jesus goes to the Father and we see Him no more; of judgment, because the ruler of this world is judged" (John 16:8-11). Through the conviction of the Holy Spirit God offers His grace to us that through faith we might be saved.
3. v. 30-31: Working of Judgment
In the past some men have tried to take judgment into their own hands. God has not given individuals the right to pass judgment upon his fellow man. (This does not deal with the governments right to judge.)

a. Father's Right = "Vengeance is Mine"

God has reserved the right to judge unto Himself. In Romans 12:19-21 we are informed:

"Beloved, do not avenge yourselves, but rather give place to wrath; for it is written, Vengeance is Mine, I will repay, says the Lord. Therefore if your enemy is hungry, feed him; if he is thirsty, give him a drink; for in so doing you will heap coals of fire on his head. Do not be overcome by evil, but overcome evil with good."

b. Future Judgment by the Son {"The LORD"}

"The Father judges no man, but hath committed all judgment unto the Son: That all *men* should honor the Son, even as they honor the Father. He that honors not the Son honors not the Father which hath sent him. Verily, verily, I say unto you, He that heareth my word, and believeth on him that sent me, hath everlasting life, and shall not come into condemnation; but is passed from death unto life. Verily, verily, I say unto you, The hour is coming, and now is, when the dead shall hear the voice of the Son of God: and they that hear shall live. For as the Father hath life in himself; so hath he given to the Son to have life in himself; and hath given him authority to execute judgment also, because he is the Son of man" (John 5:22-27).

c. "Fearful Thing to fall into the hands of the living God"

God is alive! Jesus is alive! The Holy Spirit is alive! It is a fearful thing to fall into the hand of the living God when we have unforgiven sin in our lives. Jesus said that He was coming back: When He comes this time He will not be coming as the suffering Savior, He will be coming as the Judge of all the earth.

B. v. 32-34: Receiving of Faith
  1. Struggles with Sufferings
      Jesus said: "If the world hates you, you know that it hated Me before it hated you" (John 15:18).
    a. Illumination
        This phrase "after you were illuminated" refers to the time when they had accepted the gospel message of Jesus Christ. In this one must know "the Holy Scriptures, which are able to make one wise for salvation through faith which is in Christ Jesus" (2 Timothy 3:15).
    b. Inclusion – "endured"
        Having accepted Jesus Christ in the free pardon of sin offered through His shed blood upon the cross of Calvary we will have to "endure" the blessings and the tribulations that accompany salvation.
    c. Intensity – "great struggle with sufferings"
        There are great blessings associated with becoming a Christian. There are also a "great struggle with sufferings" associated with becoming a Christian. In the world's eyes Christians are …
  2. Spectacles of Scorn
    a. Accusations – "reproaches"
        "If you are reproached for the name of Christ, blessed are you, for the Spirit of glory and of God rests upon you. … If anyone suffers as a Christian, let him not be ashamed, but let him glorify God in this matter" (1 Peter 4:14 & 16).
    b. Anguish – "tribulations"
        "Having a good conscience, when *the world* defames you as evildoers, those who revile your good conduct in Christ may be *put to shame*" (1 Peter 3:16).
    c. Associations – "became companions of those who were so treated"
        "Therefore let those who suffer according to the will of God commit their souls to Him in doing good, as to a faithful Creator" (1 Peter 4:19).

3. Sharing of the Splendid
    God has called us to "bear one another's burdens and so fulfill the law of Christ" (Galatians 6:2). We can do this when we have a proper attitude concerning life which is expressed when we …
    a. Empathetic Personality – "compassion on me"
        We are called upon to care for one another. We are to show the mercy of Jesus toward our fellow brothers and sisters in Christ. "Freely ye have received, freely give" (Matthew 10:8).
    b. Endure the Plundering of our goods
        When the world takes away the material goods that we as Christians have we are to understand that "the things which are seen *are* temporal; but the things which are not seen *are* eternal" (2 Corinthians 4:18). We must also understand that Jesus taught us to: "Take heed and beware of covetousness, for one's life does not consist in the abundance of the things he possesses" (Luke 12:15).
    c. Enduring Possession … in heaven
        Therefore "do not lay up for yourselves treasures on earth, where moth and rust destroy and where thieves break in and steal; but lay up for yourselves treasures in heaven, where neither moth nor rust destroys and where thieves do not break in and steal. For where your treasure is, there your heart will be also" (Matthew 6:19-21).
C. v. 35-39: Reward of the Faithful
    "Now he that hath wrought us for the selfsame thing *is* God, who also hath given unto us the earnest of the Spirit. Therefore *we are* always confident, knowing that, whilst we are at home in the body, we are absent from the Lord: (For we walk by faith, not by sight:)" (2 Corinthians 5:5-7). We can live with this confidence when we live, not by sight, but by the …
    1. v. 35: Promises of God
        We live in the promises of God when we live by the …

      a. Principles of – "therefore"
            Here we are pointed back to everything that has been taught in Hebrews. We are thus encouraged to live by the standards of God that we have been taught.
      b. Preserved – "cast not away"
            "Being confident of this very thing, that He (God) which has begun a good work in you will perform *it* until the day of Jesus Christ" (Philippians 1:6).
      c. Prize – "which has great reward"
            "Whatsoever ye do, do *it* heartily, as to the Lord, and not unto men; knowing that of the Lord ye shall receive the reward of the inheritance: for ye serve the Lord Christ" (Colossians 3:23-24).
  2. v. 36-37: Pattern of Good
        We are encouraged to be persistent in following the pattern of faith that has been given to us. This persistence in seen in our ...
      a. Practice of Faith –"after ye have done the will of God"
            "I beseech you therefore, brethren, by the mercies of God, that ye present your bodies a living sacrifice, holy, acceptable unto God, *which is* your reasonable service. And be not conformed to this world: but be ye transformed by the renewing of your mind, that ye may prove what *is* that good, and acceptable, and perfect, will of God" (Romans 12:1-2).
      b. Promise – "receive the promise
            "Beloved, now we are children of God; and it has not yet been revealed what we shall be, but we know that when He is revealed, we shall be like Him, for we shall see Him as He is. And everyone who has this hope in Him purifies himself, just as He is pure" (1 John 3:2-3).

    c. Preview – v. 37: "For yet a little while, and He who is coming will come and will not tarry."
    We live in expectation of the coming of our Lord Jesus Christ. "But of that day and hour no one knows, not even the angels of heaven, but *The* Father only. Therefore you also be ready, for the Son of Man is coming at an hour you do not expect" (Matthew 24:36 & 44).
3. v. 38-39: Permanent Guarantee
    John gave the reason that he wrote his letter to the church by informing us that: "These things I have written to you who believe in the name of the Son of God, that you may know that you have eternal life, and that you may *continue to* believe in the name of the Son of God. Now this is the confidence that we have in Him" (1 John 5:13-14). This confidence is seen when we have the …
    a. Perception in the Savior – "live by faith"
    Paul expressed the faith that we are to live by when he shared: "I have been crucified with Christ; it is no longer I who live, but Christ lives in me; and the *life* which I now live in the flesh I live by faith in the Son of God, who loved me and gave Himself for me" (Galatians 2:20).
    b. Pleasure of the Sovereign – "not drawback"
    The Christian's goal is to live in such a way that in the end we will hear Jesus say: "Well done, *thou* good and faithful servant: thou hast been faithful over a few things, I will make thee ruler over many things: enter thou into the joy of thy Lord" (Matthew 25:21).
    c. Permanence of the Soul – v. 39: "But we are not of those who draw back to perdition, but of those who believe to the saving of the soul."
    We have the promise that "the God of all grace, who has called us unto his eternal glory by Christ Jesus, after that ye have suffered a while, make you perfect, stablish, strengthen, settle *you*" (1 Peter 5:10).

XXI. v. 11:1 – 12:4: The Unequivocal Following of The Lordship of Christ

*. v. 1-3: Pureness of Faith
  1. v. 1: Defined
  2. v. 2: Design of
  3. v. 3: Dedication to

A. v. 4-28: Patriarchs of Faith
  1. v. 4-7: Developed Faith
    a. Obtained Witness – Abel
    b. Offered Testimony – Enoch
    c. Obedient Soul - Noah
  2. v. 8-22: Directed Faith
    a. v. 8-12: Faith based on Promises
    b. v. 13-16: Following of Pilgrims
    c. v. 17-22: Focused on the Prophecies
  3. v. 23-28: Devoted Faith
    a. v. 23: Generational Faith
    b. v. 24-27: Guiding Faith
    c. v. 28 (29): Guarding Faith

B. v. 29-40: People of Faith
  1. v. 29-31: Partakers of the Blessings
    a. Escaping Company – Israel & the mixed company
    b. Enemy of the Country – residence of Jericho
    c. Encourager of the Camp – Rahab & family
  2. v. 32-34: Prophets of God Believed
    a. Vision – Work
      (1). National Involvement – "subdued kingdoms"
      (2). Necessary Ingredient – "wrought righteousness"
      (3). Needful Insight – "obtained promises"
    b. Voice – Witness
      (1). Personal Devotion – "stopped the mouths of lions"
      (2). Public Decisions – "quenched the violence of fire"
      (3). Perceived Dedication – "escaped the edge of the sword"
    c. Victory – Warfare
      (1). Confidence – "out of weakness were made strong"
      (2). Courage – "waxed valiant in battle"
      (3). Conquered – "turned to flight the armies …"
  3. v. 35-38: Performance of The Believers

      a. v. 35: Believers' Dedicated Spouses Faithful
      b. v. 36: Beaten Down Spirits
      c. v. 37a: Bodies Destroyed Savagely
      d. v. 37b: Beleaguered-Downtrodden Souls
      e. v. 38: Better-Than the Sinners (world)
    *. v. 39-40: Promises Not Yet Belonging
      a. v. 39a: Satisfying Presentation Detailed
      b. v. 39b: Still Pressing-On in Death
      c. v. 40a: Spirit-Provided Deliverance
      d. v. 40b: Shared Perfection Developed
C. v. 12:1-3: Pattern of Faith
  1. v. 1a: The Witnesses (Hebrews 11)
    a. Patriarchs
    b. Prophets
    c. Present (v. 40)
  2. v. 1b: The Work
    a. Ready – "lay aside every weight"
    b. Resist Sin – "and the sin which does so easily beset us"
    c. Run The Set Race – "and let us run with patience the race that is set before us.
  3. v. 2-4: The Worshipful
    a. Example – Jesus Christ
      (1). Source of our Faith
        "the author and finisher of our faith"
      (2). Savior of our Faith
        "who for the joy that was set before Him endured the cross, despising the shame"
      (3). Sovereign of our Faith
        "and has sat down at the right hand of the throne of God"
    b. v. 3a: Enduring –
    "for consider Him that endured such contradiction of sinners against Himself.
    c. v. 3b-4: Exhortation –
    "lest ye be wearied and faint in your minds. You have not yet resisted to bloodshed, striving against sin."

****

XXI. v. 11:1 – 12:4: The Unequivocal Following of
The Lordship of Christ
When one decides to follow Christ for real, that commitment will be complete and unchangeable. We see this kind of commitment in the following:
*. v. 1-3: Pureness of Faith
Pure faith is ...
1. v. 1: Defined
Faith is a confident assurance that gives substance and realization of things hoped for and being the proof of things we do not see and the conviction of their reality – perceiving as real what is not revealed to the senses.
2. v. 2: Design of
It is by this kind of faith that the men of old won God's approval.
3. v. 3: Dedication to
It is faith that enables us to perceive that the whole scheme of time, space, and the cosmos were created, beautifully coordinated, and now exist at God's Word.
A. v. 4-28: Patriarchs of Faith
1. v. 4-7: Developed Faith
Faith was a growing process. God chose to give spiritual knowledge through a progressive process.
a. v. 4: Obtained Witness – Abel
Faith made Abel's sacrifice greater in the sight of God than Cain's, through which he had witness borne to him that he was upright and in right standing with God. God Himself establishing the testimony by accepting his gifts and it is by the example of his faith that Abel, though dead, continues to speak.
b. v. 5-6: Offered Testimony – Enoch
Enoch gave us the testimony that apart from faith it is impossible to be well-pleasing unto God for nobody reaches God's presence until he has learned to believe.

   c. v. 7: Obedient Soul – Noah
     Prompted by faith Noah, being forewarned of God concerning events of which as yet there was no visible sign, reverently constructed an ark to save his household. This action of faith condemned the unbelief of the rest of the world, and he became the one that God accepted as heir of the righteousness which is by faith.
2. v. 8-22: Directed Faith
  a. v. 8-12: Faith based on Promises
     We see here Abraham's family being lead by the promises that were given to him. They left their ancestral home and set out for The Place of Promise. The promise that they believed in that changed their lives was when God informed Abraham to …
> "Get out of your country, from your family and from your father's house, to a land that I will show you. I will make you a great nation; I will bless you and make your name great; and you shall be a blessing. I will bless those who bless you, and I will curse him who curses you; and in you all the families of the earth shall be blessed" (Genesis 12:1-3).

  b. v. 13-16: Following of Pilgrims
     These people all died victoriously as a result of their faith; although not having received the tangible fulfillment of the promises, they glimpsed the fulfillment of them in the distance and embraced them with delight.
  c. v. 17-22: Focused on the Prophecies
     All of the Patriarchs based their decisions upon and lived their lives in respect to the prophecies that God had given them. This is what sets them apart from the nonbeliever and the average Christian.
3. v. 23-28: Devoted Faith
     Moses' example has been given to us that we might understand how faith is passed from one generation to the next.

      a. v. 23: Generational Faith
         The story of Moses actually starts with his parents' faith. They had enough faith to keep them from being afraid of worldly leaders and to do what was right in the face of huge pressure to do the wrong thing.
      Remember that it was Moses' own mother that raised him as a nurse for Pharaoh's daughter. During that time she would have taught Moses about faith in the "God with no name" who had promised to deliver them and take them to the place designated by God.
      b. v. 24-27: Guiding Faith
         Moses had seven qualities of which we should have today as we strive to live for God.
           (1). He made a CHOICE – "choosing"
           (2). He CONSIDERED his Action – "esteeming"
           (3). He CHERISHED the truth of God over the falsehood of the world – "he had respect"
           (4). He had COURAGE – "not fearing"
           (5). He was CONSISTENT – "endured"
           (6). He COMPREHENDED – "seeing Him who"
           (7). He CELEBRATED God – "kept the Passover"
      c. v. 28 (29): Guarding Faith
         Moses passed his faith to the Children of Israel. It was a great struggle to do so, but Moses remained faithful and continued to teach the people of God for over 40 years.
B. v. 29-40: People of Faith
    We learn here that God desires to bless every nation of people in fulfilling the promise He made to Abraham "that in him all the families of the earth would be blessed."
  1. v. 29-31: Partakers of the Blessings
      Those that have faith will be receivers of the blessings of God no matter their background.
    a. Escaping Company – Israel & the mixed company
    b. Enemy of the Country – Residence of Jericho
    c. Encourager of the Camp – Rahab & family

2. v. 32-34: Prophets of God Believed

"What more shall I say? For the time would fail me to tell of…" the many prophets of God. However we can see the nature of their faith in their …
- a. Vision – Work
  - (1). National Involvement – "subdued kingdoms"
  - (2). Necessary Ingredient – "wrought righteousness"
  - (3). Needful Insight – "obtained promises"
- b. Voice – Witness
  - (1). Personal Devotion – "stopped the mouths of lions"
  - (2). Public Decisions – "quenched the violence of fire"
  - (3). Perceived Dedication – "escaped the edge of the sword"
- c. Victory – Warfare
  - (1). Confidence – "out of weakness were made strong"
  - (2). Courage – "waxed valiant in battle"
  - (3). Conquered – "turned to flight the armies …"

3. v. 35-38: Performance of The Believers

Not only are we given the example of the prophets, but we are given the example of others that were not named but were just as faithful as they. We see their faith in that …
- a. v. 35: Believers' Dedicated Spouses Faithful
- b. v. 36: Beaten Down Spirits
- c. v. 37a: Bodies Destroyed Savagely
- d. v. 37b: Beleaguered-Downtrodden Souls
- e. v. 38: Better-Than the Sinners (world)

*. v. 39-40: Promises Not Yet Belonging

Yet none of these received the promise of the coming Messiah. Even so they were given a …
- a. v. 39a: Satisfying Presentation Detailed
  "having obtained a good testimony through faith"
- b. v. 39b: Still Pressing-On in Death
  "not having received the promise"
- c. v. 40a: Spirit-Provided Deliverance
  "God having provided something better for us"
- d. v. 40b: Shared Perfection Developed
  "that they should not be made perfect apart from us"

C. v. 12:1-3: Pattern of Faith
   The pattern of faith that we should follow is seen in the ..
   1. v. 1a: The Witnesses (Hebrews 11)
      As we studied the last chapter we learned of the faith and lives of the …
      a. Patriarchs (v. 4-22)
      b. Prophets (v. 23-39)
      c. Present (v. 40)
   2. v. 1b: The Work
      Because of what we have learned about faith and the lives of believers in God we should be always be …
      a. Ready – "lay aside every weight"
      b. Resist Sin – "and the sin which does so easily beset us"
      c. Run The Set Race – "and let us run with patience the race that is set before us.
   3. v. 2-4: The Worshipful
      We can learn much from our forefathers in the faith and from the experiences that we have while striving to live obediently to our Heavenly Father. But let us consider the best that we can learn from which is our …
      a. Example – Jesus Christ
         (1). Source of our Faith
              "the author and finisher of our faith"
         (2). Savior of our Faith
              "who for the joy that was set before Him endured the cross, despising the shame"
         (3). Sovereign of our Faith
              "and has sat down at the right hand of the throne of God"
      b. v. 3a: Enduring –
         "for consider Him that endured such contradiction of sinners against Himself.
      c. v. 3b-4: Exhortation –
         "lest ye be wearied and faint in your minds. You have not yet resisted to bloodshed, striving against sin."
         Therefore, be not weary in well doing, for in due season you shall receive your reward if you faint not.

XXII. v. 12:5-17: The Validation of
The Lordship of Christ

Intro. Explanation For The Chastening of The Lord
- *. 1 Corinthians 11:31-32: "For if we would judge ourselves, we should not be judged. But when we are judged, we are chastened of the Lord, that we should not be condemned with the world."
  1. Lack of Self-Judgment
  2. Love of The Lord
  3. Lifted-Up Above the World – "not condemned with"

*. How Can We Respond to God's Chastening

I. v. 5: Exhausted By It
  A. Disremember – "Ye have forgotten"
    1. Potential – "the exhortation which speaks unto you"
    2. Position – "as unto children"
    3. Parent – "My (God, The Father) son"
  B. Despise It –
     "despise not thou the chastening of the Lord"
  C. Debilitated By It –
     "nor faint when thou art rebuked of Him"

II. v. 6-9: Endure It – "If ye endure chastening"
  A. v. 6: Necessary –
     "For whom the Lord loves He chastens, and scourges every son whom He receives"
  B. v. 7: Need It –
     "God deals with you as with sons; for what son is he whom the Father chastens not?
  C. v. 8: Names Us as His –
     "But if ye be without chastisement, whereof all are partakers, then are ye bastards, and not sons."
  D. v. 9: Natural –
     "Furthermore we have had fathers of our flesh which corrected us, and we gave them reverence: shall we not much rather be in subjection unto the Father of spirits, and live?"

III. v. 10-11: Exercised By It
  A. Amazing Awareness –
     "but He chastens <u>for our profit</u>"

B. Acquired Absorbency –
      "That we might be <u>partakers of His holiness</u>"
   C. Assured Acceptance –
      "Now no chastening for the present seems to be joyous, but grievous"
   D. Actions Affected –
      "nevertheless afterward it <u>yields the peaceable fruit of righteousness</u> unto them which are exercised thereby"
*. v. 12-17: Expectations Produced by God's Chastening
      - "Wherefore …"
   A. v. 12-13: Course to Follow
      1. Praise of God – "Stretched Up Hands"
      2. Prayer Warrior – "Strengthened Knees"
      3. Path to Follow – "Straight Paths for the Feet"
   B. v. 14: Comfort to Share
      1. Peace – "follow peace"
      2. Participation – "with all men"
      3. Purity – "holiness, without which no man shall see the Lord"
   C. v. 15-17: Consistency/Persistence–"Looking carefully" to
      1. Promote Faith –
         "Lest any man fail of the grace of God"
      2. Preventative to Futility –
         "Let any root of bitterness spring up"
      3. v. 16-17: Protect against fornication –
         "Lest there be any fornicator or profane person"
         a. Disrespectful – "sold his birthright"
         b. Disinherited – "he was rejected"
         c. Disappointed – "no place for repentance"

****

XXII. v. 12:5-17: The Validation of
                  The Lordship of Christ
Intro. Explanation For The Chastening of The Lord
   *. 1 Corinthians 11:31-32: "For if we would judge ourselves, we should not be judged. But when we are judged, we are chastened of the Lord, that we should not be condemned with the world."

There are three reasons that we are "chastened of the Lord." The first is the lack of self-judgment. We are told that if we judge ourselves then the Lord will not have to chasten us. In other words if we will use our common sense and apply God's Word to our lives then we will correct ourselves in the things that we do. God has given us the Bible {**B**asic **I**nstructions **B**efore **L**eaving **E**arth} to learn how God expects us to live. Secondly, we are chastened by the Lord because of His love for us. Just as an earthly parent corrects their children to keep them from getting hurt God corrects us to keep us from getting hurt. Thirdly, God desires that we as His children not be "condemned with the world." God would have us to live lives of purity which will avoid the pain and suffering associated with sin.

*. How Can We Respond to God's Chastening

I. v. 5: Exhausted By It

If one does not remember that God is our Heavenly Father and that He deals with us as unto children then it is easy to "despise ... the chastening of the Lord." When we forget that we are spiritual children and not grownups we will "think more highly of ourselves then we ought to think." It then becomes easy to reject the correction of the Lord. However, when we understand that we are still growing spiritually and need to be guided we then we will not faint when we are rebuked of God.

II. v. 6-9: Endure It – "If ye endure chastening"

As Spiritual children we understand that the correction of God in our lives is ...

A. v. 6: Necessary –

"For whom the Lord loves He chastens, and scourges every son whom He receives." The chastening of the Lord is the only method that will bring about spiritual growth.

B. v. 7: Need It –
"God deals with you as with sons; for what son is he whom the Father chastens not?" We accept that we need the correction of God. It is man's pride that keeps him from allowing God's chastening to produce the spiritual growth that is desired by God. Remember that God resists the proud but gives grace to the humble.

C. v. 8: Names Us as His –
"But if ye be without chastisement, whereof all are partakers, then are ye bastards, and not sons." The seen chastisement of God in a person's life is evidence that one belongs to God. The person who can live a life of sin and not have any feelings of conviction concerning the sin gives good evidence that he are not a born again Christian.

D. v. 9: Natural –
"Furthermore we have had fathers of our flesh which corrected us, and we gave them reverence: shall we not much rather be in subjection unto the Father of spirits, and live?" It is not a strange thing that our Heavenly Father disciplines us as His children when we are disobedience.

So with only this understanding we will be able to "endure" the chastening of the Lord but will not learn as much as we possibly could.

III. v. 10-11: Exercised By It

The best way to deal with the chastening of the Lord in our lives is to be "exercised by it." Just as our muscles improve with exercise so our spirituality will become stronger when we are exercised by the correction of the Lord. We will be exercised by the Lord's correction when we have an …

A. Amazing Awareness –
"He chastens <u>for our profit</u>" We must understand that everything that God allows into our lives is for our own good. For "we know that all things work together for good to those who love God, to those who are the called according to His purpose" (Romans 8:28).

B. Acquired Absorbency –
   God desires "That we might be <u>partakers of His holiness.</u>" When we understand the reason that God allows things into our lives that are uncomfortable we will focus on our personal spiritual growth instead upon the difficulties. "Knowing that the testing of your faith produces patience and let patience have its perfect work, that you may be perfect and complete, lacking nothing" (James 1:3-4).
C. Assured Acceptance –
   "Now no chastening for the present seems to be joyous, but grievous." As one experiences the testing of their faith discomfort will be felt. However this discomfort will lead to a deeper understanding of God and spiritual things. A Christian is willing to experience these "spiritual valleys" because they know it will lead to "spiritual mountain tops."
D. Actions Affected –
   "nevertheless afterward it <u>yields the peaceable fruit of righteousness</u> unto them which are exercised thereby"
   When one allows the chastisement of the Lord to work in their life the end result will be the "fruit of righteousness." God is striving to make us new creatures in Christ which exhibits the qualities of Jesus giving witness to the life changing power of the Holy Spirit.

*. v. 12-17: Expectations Produced by God's Chastening
   - "Wherefore …" the seen results of one that has been exercised by the chastening of God are expressed when that Christian has a …
A. v. 12-13: Course to Follow
   The spiritually minded Christian will be one that loves to praise God in worship. The "stretched up hands" refer to one whom focuses upon the great characteristics of our Heavenly Father. The recognition will lead this individual to become a prayer warrior spending time bowed before our all powerful God. Having God as one's central focus and spending time in

prayer will help this one to identify the path that has been set before him to walk. This one will find spiritual healing for a right understanding concerning the leadership of God.

B. v. 14: Comfort to Share

The Christian's spirituality will be seen in the fact of being the "peacemakers of God. For they will be called the children of God" (Matthew 5:9). This one will "as much as depends upon him live peaceably with all men. Not being overcome by evil, but overcoming evil with the goodness" of holiness (Romans 12:18 & 21). This witness will allow others to see God in them.

C. v. 15-17: Consistency/Persistence

The spiritual Christian will "Look carefully" to

1. Promoting Faith –

"Lest any man fail of the grace of God"

This phrase here does not refer to one that has lost his salvation (as some would teach). Based upon what has come before we understand that this statement simply means one that has failed to live up to the expectation of the Christian life. As one grows spiritually a concern about living according to Christ's standards become paramount. Therefore the spiritual Christian strives to live and to "walk by faith and not by sight."

2. Preventative to Futility –

"Lest any root of bitterness spring up"

The spiritual Christian will do everything possible to not allow bitterness to enter in their heart. We understand that bitterness is the first step in a downward spiral which ends in destruction. For "bitterness leads to wrath, wrath leads to anger, anger leads to clamor (yelling or screaming), clamor leads to evil speaking, and evil speaking leads to malice (malevolent actions) which we should be put away from us," (Ephesians 4:31).

3. v. 16-17: Protect against Fornication –
   "Lest there be any fornicator or profane person"
The spiritual Christian will also strive to live with the right priorities in life and not be like Esau. Esau is described as a fornicator and profane person because of his disrespect for the important things in life. He sold his birthright for a bowl of lentil soup without regard to the consequences. The result of his selfish action was that he was disinherited. His cry to Israel was "Bless me, even me also!" His actions led to him being disappointed in what blessing his father could give him. He "found no place for repentance, though he sought it diligently with tears." Sometimes the consequences of our actions cannot be turned aside. Remember that one can choose their actions; but one does not have the option of choosing the consequences of those actions. This is taught in the Biblical concept of "what you sow, you shall reap."

**XXIII. v. 12:18-29: The Worship Places of
The Lordship of Christ**
- A. v. 18-21: Mountain of Fear
  1. Physical Place
  2. Prohibited Place
  3. Promising Place
- B. v. 22-24: Mountain of Faith
  1. Site of Power –
     – "to Mount Zion to the city of the living God"
  2. Spiritual Place –
     – "to an innumerable company of angels"
  3. Saved Persons –
     – "to the general assembly and church of the firstborn who are registered in heaven"
  4. Sovereign Potentate –
     – "to God the Judge of all"
  5. Spirits Perfected –
     – "to the spirits of just men made perfect"
  6. Savior of Permanence –
     – "to Jesus the Mediator of the new covenant"
  7. sprinkling Pointing to Better Promises –
     – "to the blood of sprinkling that speaks better things than that of Abel"
- C. v. 25-29: Mountain of Fire
  1. v. 25: a place of Reception {not to be Refused}
  2. v. 26: a place of Respect
  3. v. 27: a place of Removal
  4. v. 27: a place of Remaining
  5. v. 28: a place of Receiving
  6. v. 28: a place of Reverence and godly fear
  7. v. 29: a place of Recognition –
     "For our God is a consuming fire"

****

XXIII. v. 12:18-29: The Worship Places of
The Lordship of Christ

In the distant past up unto our present day places of worship have been described in different ways. Here we will look at three different venues that have been dedicated as places of worship unto the Lord our God.

A. v. 18-21: Mountain of Fear – Worship by the Body

This was the mountain upon which God placed the Ten Commandments into Moses' hands to give to the chosen people of Israel. It was a physical mountain which we call Mount Sinai. The place where this mountain is located is in Median on the West side of the Gulf of Aqaba. This was a place that God had appointed for the worship of Himself. It was also a place that had been prohibited to approach in an unprepared manner. "if so much as a breast touches the mountain, it was to be stoned or shot with an arrow." The People of God were to learn that God is holy and could not be approached in a disrespectful manner. Even so, this mountain was a place of Promise. God had purposed to give forth His blessings to His people if they would only obey Him. Here God gave them a law which could be obeyed in the body. God desires us to worship Him with our mortal bodies by surrendering ourselves to His will.

B. v. 22-24: Mountain of Faith – Worship by The Mind

Here we have our focus directed toward worshiping God with our conscience mind. We decide to worship God when we recognize and accept ...

1. Site of Power –

– "to Mount Zion to the city of the living God"

"Mount Zion" represented a place of power and control. The mental process of worshiping God must begin with His omnipresence, omniscience, omnipotence. One must recognize that God is in total control and that we are nothing in His presence. For without Him we can do nothing.

2. Spiritual Place –
   – "to an innumerable company of angels"
   Next we need to understand that we are living in a spiritual world. We do not simply live in a materialistic realm where everything can be explained by natural processes.
3. Saved Persons –
   – "to the general assembly and church of the firstborn who are registered in heaven"
   Jesus said that He came to build His Church. Although the "Church" has problems {because it is made up of imperfect humans} it is still Jesus' Church. We have been commanded not to "forsake the assembling of ourselves together, as the manner of some *are*." One makes an intentional decision as to whether congregational worship is to be important to them or not. To refuse to worship with the Church is to refuse to worship God mentally.
4. Sovereign Potentate –
   – "to God the Judge of all"
   We also give reference and worship God when we comprehend that "we must all appear before the judgment seat of Christ, that each one may receive the things done in the body, according to what has been done, whether good or bad" (2 Corinthians 5:10).
5. Spirits Perfected –
   – "to the spirits of just men made perfect"
   We worship God mentally when we realize that when "we confess our sins God is faithful and just to forgive us our sins and to cleanse us from all unrighteousness" (1 John 1:9). Then we become "God's workmanship, created in Christ Jesus for good works, which God prepared beforehand that we should walk in them" (Ephesians 2:10). "For this reason ... we are not ashamed, for we know in whom we have believed and am persuaded that he is able to keep what we have committed to Him until that Day" (2 Timothy 1:12).

6. Savior of Permanence –
   – "to Jesus the Mediator of the new covenant"
   We also worship God in our acceptance that Jesus is "the way, the truth, and the life. No one comes to the Father except through Him" (John 14:6). "There is one God and one Mediator between God and men, the Man Christ Jesus, who gave Himself a ransom for all, to be testified in due time" (1 Timothy 2:5-6).
7. sprinkling Pointing to Better Promises –
   – "to the blood of sprinkling that speaks better things than that of Abel"
   In Christ we are given better things than those whom lived under the Old Testament Covenant of the Law because of the New Covenant of Grace that is in Him. The Book of Hebrews (in part) was written to explain these new things. Here is a short summary of how …

   Christ is Better
   (1). A Better Security
      (a). v. 1:1-4: Better Revelation
         -- v. 6:9: Better things of You
      (b). v. 7:19: Better Hope
      (c). v. 7:20-28: Better Testament (Priesthood)
   (2). A Better Source
      (a). v. 8:6: Better Covenant
      (b). v. 8:6: Better Promises
      (c). v. 9:23: Better Sacrifice
   (3). A Better Satisfaction
      (a). v. 10:34: Better Possessions
      (b). v. 11:16: Better Country
      (c). v. 11:35: Better Resurrection
   (*). v. 12:24: Speaking Better Things

C. v. 25-29: Mountain of Fire-Worship by our Souls/Spirits
   It is true that we are to worship God with our bodies and with our minds; but for worship to be complete one must worship God will all the heart (the soul). We worship this way when we turn our Soul into …

1. v. 25: a place of Reception {not to be Refused}
    We must be careful that we do not refuse God who speaks to us. We have already been encouraged to contemplate "how shall we escape if we neglect so great a salvation, which at the first began to be spoken by the Lord, and was confirmed to us by those who heard Him, God also bearing witness both with signs and wonders, with various miracles, and gifts of the Holy Spirit, according to His own will?" (Hebrews 2:3-4).
2. v. 26: a place of Respect
    We must have the proper respect of God. The quote here is from Haggai 2:6-9 which says:
    > "For thus says the Lord of hosts: Once more I will shake heaven and earth, the sea and dry land; and I will shake all nations, and they shall come to the Desire of All Nations, and I will fill this temple with glory, says the Lord of hosts. ...The glory of this latter temple shall be greater than the former, says the Lord of hosts. In this place I will give peace, says the Lord of hosts."

    "Your body is the temple of the Holy Spirit who is in you, whom you have from God, and you are not your own." God will shake your soul when you give Him the proper respect and you will be given the peace of God.
3. v. 27: a place of Removal
    When God shakes your soul then the things which should not be there will be removed. God desires to remove from your life anything which is unspiritual and unprofitable for you. Just what form this "shaking" will take we do not know and may be different for every individual.
4. v. 27: a place of Remaining
    When God shakes us the spiritual things which cannot be shaken will remain. This is the way that our God cleanses us from all unrighteousness. We then will begin to experience spiritual fullness.

5. v. 28: a place of Receiving
   The word tells us that when we become part of the family of God through faith in Jesus Christ we become "joint-heirs" with Christ of the riches of heaven. True worship comes from a heart that focuses upon the Kingdom work of Christ instead of the materialistic things of this world. "If then you were raised with Christ, seek those things which are above, where Christ is, sitting at the right hand of God. Set your mind on things above, not on things on the earth" (Colossians 3:1-2).
6. v. 28: a place of Reverence and Godly fear
   The expression of our worship is seen in the acceptable service that we render to God. Thus we are directed "brethren, by the mercies of God, that we present our bodies as living sacrifices, holy, acceptable to God, which is our reasonable service. And that we do not conform to this world, but are transformed by the renewing of our mind, that we may prove what is that good and acceptable and perfect will of God" (Romans 12:1-2).
7. v. 29: a place of Recognition –
   "For our God is a consuming fire"
   Worship comes out of a right understanding of the nature of God. God's Character Resume is found in Romans 11:33-36. Here God reveals the following about Himself:
   (1). Name: God, Lord, The Almighty
   (2). Job Title: Creator & Sustainer of the Universe
   (3). Judgments: Unsearchable
   (4). Ways: Unfathomable
   (5). Mind: No one knows His mind
   (6). Counselor: No on is His counselor
   (7). Debts: He owes no debt to anyone
   (8). Relationship to All Things
       Everything that exists is   From Him
                                    Through Him and
                                    To Him.

XXIV. v. 13:1-6: The X-pectations of
The Lordship of Christ

A. v. 1-3: Hospitality of The Messengers of Christ
  1. v. 1: Encouragement
     "Let brotherly love continue"
  2. v. 2: Entertainment
     "Do not forget to entertain strangers, for by so doing some have unwittingly entertained angels."
  3. v. 3: Empathy
     "Remember the prisoners as if chained with them—those who are mistreated—since you yourselves are in the body also."
B. v. 4: Honorableness of Marriage in Christ
  1. Respected
     "Marriage is honorable among all"
  2. Responsibility
     "and the bed undefiled"
  3. Requirements
     "but fornicators and adulterers God will judge"
C. v. 5-6: How-To of Motivation by Christ
  1. Conduct
     "Let you conduct be without covetousness"
  2. Contentment
     "be content with such things as you have"
  3. v. 6: Confession
     "For He Himself has said, I will never leave you nor forsake you."

****

XXIV. v. 13:1-6: The X-pectations of
The Lordship of Christ

When one accepts Jesus Christ as Savior and makes Him Lord of life then there are certain expectations that God requires. Paul mentions many of these expectations in the lists that he gives throughout the epistles he wrote. Here we are given an instantly recognizable list of things to do in honoring Jesus as our Lord.

A. v. 1-3: Hospitality of The Messengers of Christ
   Hospitality is defined as: "The friendly reception and treatment of guests characterized by betokening warmth and generosity." Its base word is "hospital" which is a place that encourages and promotes the health of individuals. Christian hospitality is to welcome openly and to promote the spiritual health of others. We can do this when we give ...
  1. v. 1: Encouragement
  "Let brotherly love continue"
   As Christians we are part of the "Family of God." We are thus commanded to "love one another as I (Jesus) have loved you." Jesus also informed us that others would know that we are Christians in that we love one another. When we studied "the Bond of the Believers" under The Sanctuary Worship of The Lordship of Christ we learned about the necessity of love in all things that we do. We are to always promote this love of Christ in us by sharing it with our fellow believers.
  2. v. 2: Entertainment
  "Do not forget to entertain strangers, for by so doing some have unwittingly entertained angels."
   Not only are we to be hospitable toward other Christians but we are to entertain "strangers" as well. Our generosity must extend beyond our "own" circle and reach out to others. We do this in two main ways: First, we are to do this on a personal level. Individually we are call upon to share of the blessing that God has give us with those in need that are around us. Secondly, we can do this through giving to missions that will go to help people that we may never meet. Paul encourages the Christians at Philippi to give "not that he sought the gift, but that fruit would abound to their account" (Philippians 4:17). When we give to missions spiritual fruit will be accredited to us even though we never meet the ones we help.

3. v. 3: Empathy
   "Remember the prisoners as if chained with them—those who are mistreated—since you yourselves are in the body also."

   Every Christian must remember that they "have been made alive, because we were once dead in trespasses and sins, in which we once walked according in the course of this world, according to the prince of the power of the air, and we had the spirit which now works in the sons of disobedience. At one time we conducted ourselves in the lusts of our flesh, fulfilling the desires of the flesh and of the mind, and were by nature children of wrath, just as other" (Ephesians 2:1-3). "But God, who is rich in mercy, because of His great love with which He loved us, even when we were dead in trespasses, made us alive together with Christ and raised us up together, and made us to sit together in the heavenly places in Christ Jesus" (Ephesians 2:4-6). We therefore can have empathy for those that are still under the bondage of sin because we were once there ourselves. Never forget from whence you have come and to where Christ Jesus has brought you by grace.

B. v. 4: Honorableness of Marriage in Christ

   The Christian-Biblical view of sex is unique in the world we live in. We understand that man was created by God as a sexual being. However we also understand that this intimate relationship is more than physical in its totality. The sexual union is physical, mental and spiritual and must be understood in context of how God designed sex to fulfill man's total needs.

   1. Respected
   "Marriage is honorable among all"

   Let us understand that marriage has been honored in all societies of the past. Marriage and family was the first social structures that God set up for the development of mankind. Because we live in a fallen and sinful world in every culture there have always been those which disdained marriage and family; this minority has on a very few occasions taken over the social fabric of a complete culture. The end results of which have always been disastrous; one example was the cities of Sodom and Gomorrah. God would have mankind to respect and give honor to the institute of marriage.

2. Responsibility

"and the bed undefiled"

In a world where "free-sex" is promoted by the government, the entertainment culture, society in general, and by literature it is no wonder that the idea that "sex" is only for the marriage bed is considered out-of-date. Yet this intimate union was designed by God to be a physical-spiritual act. We are given to understand that when a couple engages in intercourse the two actually become "one flesh." This means that when an individual is promiscuous that person becomes "one flesh" with many others. This special union was designed to between a man and his wife joined in a monogamous relationship that is to last until "death does them part."

3. Requirements

"but fornicators and adulterers God will judge"

When marriage is dishonored, refused, and forgotten sinful actions results. Fornication is the word used in Scripture referring to "premarital sex." Adultery is the word used in Scripture referring to those which have become unfaithful to their spouse and commit sexual acts with another individual. God has made it plain that He will judge these sinful actions. God will not only judge individuals who commit such actions but He will also judge societies which condone such sins as alternative lifestyles. We must never view these acts of sin as acceptable individually or in our culture and society.

C. v. 5-6: How-To of Motivation by Christ
   As Christians we must understand that Christ has expectation of us and in how we live our lives. Our actions will be pleasing to Christ when others see Him in our ...
   1. Conduct
      "Let you conduct be without covetousness"
      It has been said that one should "practice what he preaches." In other words – one's conduct should express one's beliefs. When one lives for Christ that individual should never do so in prideful arrogance. We are commanded to live to please the Lord and not to be men-pleasers. Jesus said that we are not to be like the hypocrites, doing things so others will see us and give us personal praise, for they have their reward here on earth. We are not to live so that we might get personal acclaim but strive to bring glory to our Savior and Lord Jesus Christ. Don't be jealous of what others have or strive to attain what others have achieved. Be willing to serve in the place where God has put you and then your conduct can be without covetousness.
   2. Contentment
      "be content with such things as you have"
      In 1 Timothy 6:3-12 we are taught a lesson concerning "godliness with contentment is great gain". To receive this great gain one must have a ...
      a. v. 3-5: Christ's Servant Attitude
         To show this attitude one must have the right ...
         (1). Following – "These things teach and exhort"
         (2). Faith – "the words of our Lord Jesus Christ, and to the doctrine which is according to godliness"
         (3). Fellowship – "the proud ... from such withdraw thyself"
      b. v. 6-10 Content Satisfied Acceptance
         (1). v. 6-8: Dedication That is Requiring
            (a). Encouragement
            (b). Expectation
            (c). Essentials

(2). v. 9-10: Desire to Be Rich =
Love of Money
  (a). Guide = Temptation
  (b). Greed = Snare
  (c). Grief = Snare
    [1]. Drown = "Strayed from the faith"
    [2]. Destruction = "Pierced themselves"
    [3]. Doom = "perdition" = "many sorrows"
c. v. 11-12: Call to Spiritual Action
  (1). Fleeing The Wrong
    (a). Lusts of the Foolish
    (b). Love of The Failing
    (c). Longing for the False
  (2). Following The Right
    (a). Character – "righteousness & godliness"
    (b). Commitment – "faith & love"
    (c). Conditioning – "patience & gentleness"
  (3). Fight The Good Fight of Faith =
"lay hold on eternal life"
    (a). Call into the Ministry
    (b). Confession of the Messiah
    (c). Congregation of Messengers

3. Confession

"For He Himself has said, I will never leave you nor forsake you."

Since we comprehend that Jesus is "the friend which sticks closer than a brother" (Psalm 18:24) we can proclaim our …

  a. Confirmation – "The Lord is my helper"

This quote is from Psalm 118:6 which parallels this part with the words: "The Lord is with me." The presence of Jesus in our lives promotes our …

b. Confidence – "I will not fear"
This confidence is expressed in that (2 Timothy 1:7) "God has not given us the spirit of fear; but of …"
   (1). Prominence – "power"
   (2). Passion – "love"
   (3). Persuasiveness – "a sound mind"
This confidence promotes …
c. Courage – "What can man do to me?"
This courage is expressed in one "not being ashamed of the gospel of Christ" (Romans 1:16-17) "for it is the …
   (1). Work of Salvation
      - "it is the power of God to salvation for everyone who believes, for the Jew first and also for the Greek"
   (2). Wisdom of the Sovereign
      - "in it the righteousness of God is revealed from faith to faith"
   (3). Way of the Saved
      - "as it is written, The just shall live by faith"

XXV. v. 13:7-17: The Yard-Lines of
The Lordship of Christ
- A. v. 7-9: Remembered Direction
  - 1. v. 7: Shepherds under Christ
    "Remember those who rule over you"
    - a. Preached
      "who have spoken the word of God to you"
    - b. Patterned
      "whose faith follow"
    - c. Product
      "considering the outcome of their conduct"
  - 2. v. 8: Standard is Christ
    "Jesus Christ is the same ..."
    - a. Past – "yesterday"
    - b. Present – "today"
    - c. Proceeding to – "and forever"
  - 3. v. 9: Stability by Christ
    - a. Correct Doctrinally
      "Do not be carried about with various and strange doctrines"
    - b. Consciously Devoted
      "For it is good that the heart be established by grace"
    - c. Conscience of Distractions
      "not with foods which have not profited those who have been occupied with them"
- B. v. 10-14: Road to Discipleship
  - 1. v. 10: Outside the Beginning Ceremonies
    "We have al altar from which those who serve the tabernacle have no right to eat.
  - 2. v. 11-12: Outside the Boundaries of Commandments
    "For the bodies of those animals, whose blood is brought into the sanctuary by the high priest for sin, are burned outside the camp. Therefore Jesus also, that He might sanctify the people with His own blood, suffered outside the gate."

3. v. 13-14: Outside the Box of Comfort
"Therefore let us go forth to Him, outside the camp, bearing His reproach. For here we have no continuing city, but we seek the one to come."
C. v. 15-17: Response of Dedication
1. v. 15: Sacrifices of Praise to God
"Therefore by Him …"
a. Visual
"let us continually offer the sacrifice of praise to God"
b. Vocal
"that is, the fruit of our lips"
c. Vicarious
"giving thanks to His name"
2. v. 16: Service that Pleases God
"… for with such sacrifices God is well pleased"
a. Remember the Opportunities
"Do not forget"
b. Requirement of Obedience
"to do good"
c. Responding to Others
"and to share"
3. v. 17: Submission that Produces Grace
a. Respect for the Pastor
"Obey those who rule over you, and be submissive"
b. Responsibility of the Pastor
"for they watch out for your souls, as those who must give account."
c. Revenue from the Pastor
"Let them do so with joy and not with grief, for that would be unprofitable for you"

****

XXV. v. 13:7-17: The Yard-Lines of
The Lordship of Christ

In Christ there are some yard-lines or goals that we should desire to reach. Unless goals are set and standards are given no one will ever know if the desired destination has been reached. We can reach Christ's goals for us when we follow the right …

A. v. 7-9: Remembered Direction
> Those that have been raised with Christ are commanded to "seek those things which are above, where Christ is, sitting at the right hand of God. Set your mind on things above, not on things on the earth" (Colossians 3:1-2). To reach this high goal we are to give great respect to the ...

1. v. 7: Shepherds under Christ
> Pastors have been given charge to "shepherd the flock of God which is among them, serving as overseers, not by compulsion but willingly, not for dishonest gain but eagerly; nor as being lords over those entrusted to them, but being examples to the flock" (1 Peter 5:2-3). The Church follows the lordship of Christ by "remembering those that rule over them, who have preached to them by speaking the word of God to them, who have given them a pattern to follow and have produced godly results based upon their faith." This remembering is expressed by the honor and respect that is given to the pastor of the local church.

2. v. 8: Standard is Christ
> The fact that "Jesus Christ is the same yesterday, today, and forever" teaches us that our standards for living as a Christian never changes. If something was a sin in the past it is still a sin today. Society should not dictate the standard of right or wrong for the Christian. We are to focus upon the teachings of Jesus, the example of Jesus and the interpretation of Scripture based upon Jesus to determine what is right or wrong. The Christian must never allow personal preferences to dictate the basis for determining the godliness of some action. Just because some Christians do not like something the something should not be considered a sin or unacceptable. This should be determined based upon how the something relates to Jesus Christ and His standards. Godliness is decided by God the Father, was lived out by Jesus Christ, and convicted of through the power of The Holy Spirit as revealed in God's Word.

3. v. 9: Stability by Christ
   For the Christian to continue in the right direction that God would have us to go in one must strive to be ...
   a. Correct Doctrinally
   "Do not be carried about with various and strange doctrines"
   How does one determine what is correct doctrinally? The question is answered by Paul when he wrote the Church in Philippians 4:8-9. The things that a Christian thinks upon are to be judged based upon ...
      1. The Correctness of a Thing/is It a Lie
         (a). True
         (b). Honest
         (c). Just
      2. The Character of a Thing/is It Lewd
         (a). Pure
         (b). Lovely
         (c). of a Good Report
      3. The Consequences of a Thing/where does It Lead
         (a). If there be any virtue
         (b). If there be any praise
   For things that are thought to be accepted as doctrinally correct they must also pass the test of being ...
      1. Educated in by the Christian Community
         "which you learned"
      2. Embraced by the Christian Community
         "which you received"
      3. Evangelistically Preached by the Christian Community
         "which you have heard"
      4. Example Given by the Christian Community
         "which you saw in me"
      5. Emmanuel Based in the Christian Community
         "the God of peace will be with you"
   A belief that can pass this test is most likely one that is doctrinally correct in Jesus Christ.

    b. Consciously Devoted
"For it is good that the heart be established by grace"
To be stable in Christ the Christian must be completely devoted to the "doctrine of Christ." "Whoever tr4ansgresses and does not abide in the doctrine of Christ does not have God. He who abides in the doctrine of Christ has both the Father and the Son" (2 John 9). Jesus Christ is the only way of salvation. Anyone denying this does not have the Father.
    c. Conscience of Distractions
"not with foods which have not profited those who have been occupied with them"
The stable Christian must also refuse to let the distractions of this world interfere with their Christian walk. The Christian's focus must be upon Jesus and upon the Word of God. Christian "hearts need to be encouraged, being knit together in love, and attaining to all riches of the full assurance of understanding, to the knowledge of the mystery of God, both of the Father and of Christ, in whom are hidden all the treasures of wisdom and knowledge. Now this I say lest anyone should deceive you with persuasive words. ... Beware lest anyone cheat you through philosophy and empty deceit, according to the tradition of men, according to the basic principles of the world, and not according to Christ" (Colossians 2:2-4, 8).

B. v. 10-14: Road to Discipleship
  1. v. 10: Outside the Beginning Ceremonies
"We have an altar from which those who serve the tabernacle have no right to eat.
The whole of the book of Hebrews has been devoted to the teaching that we as Christians are not under the Old Testament Sacrificial System. Those that have remained bound to the Old Testament System and have refused to accept the sacrifice of Jesus Christ's blood do not have the right to enjoy the blessing of the New Covenant that was established in Jesus. There is no such thing as New Testament Judaism.

2. v. 11-12: Outside the Boundaries of Commandments
   "For the bodies of those animals, whose blood is brought into the sanctuary by the high priest for sin, are burned outside the camp. Therefore Jesus also, that He might sanctify the people with His own blood, suffered outside the gate."

   Here we are given a reference concerning the crucifixion of Jesus Christ and the location of that event. Two sites are held today as Calvary. The older, more traditional Church of the Holy Sepulcher is a complex of religious shrines venerated as the place of Christ's cross and tomb. The other location is called Gordon's Calvary which is outside the city and also features the face of a skull (the meaning of the word Golgotha). The point being that Jesus' death met the requirements of God for the sacrifice for the sins of the people of the earth.

3. v. 13-14: Outside the Box of Comfort
   "Therefore let us go forth to Him, outside the camp, bearing His reproach. For here we have no continuing city, but we seek the one to come."

   Therefore we are to seek Christ "outside the box" of the Old Testament Sacrificial System for that system does not continue. In this we must accept that there are costs involved in being a disciple of Christ. Some of these costs are found in Luke 14:26-35. Jesus lists at least seven costs that is required of those that would be His disciples:

   (1). v. 26: Priorities
      (a). Decision – "if anyone come to Me"
      (b). Dedication – "and hate not his …"
         [the concerns that we cannot place before Christ are …]
         [1]. Respectful – "father and mother"
         [2]. Responsibility – "wife and children"
         [3]. Relations – "brothers and sisters"
         [*]. our Rights – "yes, your own life also"
      (c). Discipleship – "be my disciples"

(2). v. 27: Passions
   (a). Cross – "bear his cross"
   (b). Come – "come after Me"
   (c). Commitment – "to be My disciple"
(3). v. 28-30: Price (our sacrifice)
   (a). Intentions – "intended to build"
   (b). Intelligence – "count the cost"
   (c). Investment – "whether he has enough"
(4). v. 31-32: Pride given up
   (a). Accept our Limitations – king considered
   (b). Acknowledge our Inabilities – king understood
   (c). Ask for Help – king asked for help
(5). v. 33: Poverty
   (a). Will – v. 28: "our intentions"
   (b). Wants – v. 31: "as our own king"
   (c). Worth – "forsake all"
(6). v. 34-35a: Performance – "ye are salt"
   (a). Preserve The Good (truth)
   (b). Protects The Godly (underfoot = melts ice)
   (c). Presents The Gospel – gives flavor to life
(7). v. 35b: Perception
   (a). Listen – "he that has an ear"
   (b). Learn – "let him listen"
   (c). Live

The whole point of "listening" and "learning" is to "LIVE" what we have listened to and have learned. To be a DISCIPLE OF CHIRST we must 'LIVE BY FAITH OF THE SON OF GOD, JESUS CHRIST."

C. v. 15-17: Response of Dedication

When someone is truly dedicated to Jesus Christ that individual's life will show signs of that dedication. Three of those signs are …

1. v. 15: Sacrifices of Praise to God
"Therefore by Him …"

In Christ the Christian will give visible evidence that praises God. Christianity is a faith which produces verifiable evidence of one's commitment to God in Christ Jesus. The praise will also be verbal. For the

sacrifices of praise unto God is the "fruit of our lips." For "God's Word *should be in our* heart like a burning fire, shut up in our bones; *which makes us* weary with not speaking of God and therefore we cannot refrain from speaking" (Jeremiah 20:9). The great desire to give praise to God is brought about because of our thankful hearts for who He is and what he has done for us in Christ Jesus. In this we can give vicarious worship to God the Father.
2. v. 16: Service that Pleases God
"… for with such sacrifices God is well pleased." Knowing this encourages us to never forget the opportunities that we are given to be obedient to God in doing good for those that are around us. To one day hear our heavenly Father say to us: "Well done thou good and faithful servant, enter ye in unto the rest of your Lord" is the greatest desire of a child of God.
3. v. 17: Submission that Produces Grace
Based upon this love for our heavenly Father we must understand that He desires us to give the proper respect and honor due His representatives = Pastors. God has set godly men in places as overseers of His Church in this world. These Men have dedicated their entire lives to the service of God and His people. If a church has the confidence to call a man to be their pastor then that church should have the same confidence to follow his leadership as their pastor. The pastor's main responsibility is to "watch out for your souls, as those who must give account" to God for the work that is done. Remember, pastors are pictured in the right hand of Christ: signifying that no man can hurt them without Christ's displeasure and no man can save them if they disobey Christ's commands. The pastor's greatest revenue is when he can lead the flock of God "with joy and not grief, which would be unprofitable for the church." Therefore, give the proper honor and respect to the man of God that leads your church as a shepherd under Christ, the Chief Shepherd.

**XXVI. v. 13:18-21: The Zone of
              The Lordship of Christ**
  A. v. 18-19: Prayer Motivated
       "pray for us"
    1. Good Conduct
       "for we are confident that we have a good conscience"
    2. Gracious Character
       "in all things desiring to live honorably"
    3. Guided Course
       "but I especially urge you to do this, that I may be restored to you the sooner"
  B. v. 20: Providential Maker
       "Now may the God of peace who …"
    1. Sovereign of Salvation (peace)
       "brought up our Lord Jesus from the dead"
    2. Shepherd of The Sheep
       "our Lord Jesus … that great Shepherd of the sheep"
    3. Savior of Souls
       "through the blood of the everlasting covenant"
  C. v. 21: Personality in the Making
    1. Complete in every Good Work
    2. Conditioned to do God's Will
       "to do His will, working in you what is well pleasing in His sight"
    3. Christ-Centered for Glorifying Worship
       "through Jesus Christ, to whom be glory forever and ever. Amen"

****

XXVI. v. 13:18-21: The Zone of
              The Lordship of Christ
  A. v. 18-19: Prayer Motivated
       As the author begins to close his encouragements to his readers he asks for them to pray for him. The writer had evidently lived among his readers for a time and they knew him very well. Whoever wrote this epistle, be it written by Paul, Apollos, or by someone else the readers where familiar with him. The writer was

confident that his readers knew of his good conduct and he also had a good conscience concerning his actions while among the readers. A Christian should always strive to have a gracious character which gives testimony to the work of Jesus Christ in their life. Our character as a Christian should always be lived honorably. The writers desire for the prayers of the readers what that he would be able to once again be among them in person. This might indicate that this epistle was written by Paul while he was in prison at Rome (as some suggest).

"pray for us"

B. v. 20: Providential Maker

A prayer for a blessing is here begun. It must be understood that if one is to have a true blessing that blessing must come from the God of the Bible (the God of Peace). For "every good gift and every perfect gift is from above, and comes down from the Father of lights, with whom there is no variation or shadow of turning" (James 1:17). The only true blessing of peace that one can have must come from the Sovereign of Salvation (God) which "brought up our Lord Jesus from the dead." To be saved one "must confess with their mouth the Lord Jesus and believe in their heart that God has raised Him from the dead" (Romans 10:9). Jesus has come to be the Shepherd of His Sheep. Jesus said: "I am the good shepherd, and know my *sheep*, and am known of mine. As the Father knows me, even so know I the Father: and I lay down my life for the sheep. My sheep hear my voice, and I know them, and they follow me: And I give unto them eternal life; and they shall never perish, neither shall any *man* pluck them out of my hand. My Father, which gave *them* me, is greater than all; and no *man* is able to pluck *them* out of my Father's hand. I and *my* Father are one" (John 10:14-15, 27-30). Jesus came to save our souls "through the blood of the everlasting covenant which He shed upon the cross of Calvary."

C. v. 21: Personality in the Making

    The blessing continues by giving a description of just what God would do in the lives of His people. God desires to make us complete in every good work as we become conditioned to do His will while keeping our focus upon Christ. Paul encouraged the Philippians when he wrote to them (v. 2:12-16): "Wherefore, my beloved, as ye have always obeyed, not as in my presence only, but now much more in my absence, work out your own salvation with fear and trembling. For it is God which works in you both to will and to do of *his* good pleasure. Do all things without murmurings and disputings: That ye may be blameless and harmless, the sons of God, without rebuke, in the midst of a crooked and perverse nation, among whom ye shine as lights in the world; Holding forth the word of life; that I may rejoice in the day of Christ, that I have not run in vain, neither labored in vain." Here we see that God desires us to do the work that proves our salvation and to do the work which fulfills His good pleasure for us. Our ultimate goal is to be pleasing to our Savior and Lord Jesus Christ.

XXVII. v. 13:22-25: The ABC of
The Lordship of Christ
- A. v. 22: Appeal
  "and I appeal to you"
  1. Brethren of Witness
     "brethren"
  2. Bear the Word
     "bear with the word of exhortation"
  3. Brief Writing
     "for I have written to you in few words"
- B. v. 23: Brotherhood
  1. Fellowship of Discipleship
     "know that <u>our</u> brother Timothy"
  2. Focus Delivered
     "has been set free"
  3. Future Desired
     "with whom I shall see you if he comes shortly"
- C. v. 24-25: Conversations
  1. Shared
     "greet all that rule over you and the saints"
  2. Sent
     "Those from Italy greet you"
  3. Source
     "Grace be with you all. Amen"

****

XXVII. v. 13:22-25: The ABC of
The Lordship of Christ

A. v. 22: Appeal – "and I appeal to you"

As the writer ends his treatise on the Lordship of Christ he appeals to them as the brethren of witness. We must understand that God through Jesus Christ has called us to be His witnesses. The readers are encouraged to bear the Word of exhortation even if it is hard to take in the brief writing. As individuals that have made Jesus Christ our Lord we are encouraged to remember that in Christ we are given a new life and a

new focus. In 2 Corinthians 5:17-21 the dimensions of this life are laid out:
1. v. 17: The POSSIBILITY of Being in Christ
   a. OFFER in Christ – "therefore if"
   b. OPPORTUNITY of Christ – "any man"
   c. ONLY WAY is Christ – "be in Christ"
2. v. 17b: The PRODUCT of Being in Christ
   a. PARTAKING of Christ
      – "he is a new creature"
   b. PUTTING OFF because of Christ
      – "old things are passed away"
   c. POINT-of-VIEW through Christ
      – "behold, all things are become new"
3. v. 18: The PURPOSE of Being in Christ
   a. Having a NEW CENTER OF ALL
      – "and all things are of God"
   b. Being in a NEW CONDITION
      – "who has reconciled us to Himself by Jesus Christ"
   c. Receiving a NEW CALLING
      – "and has given to us the ministry of reconciliation"
*. v. 19-21: The POSITION of Being in Christ
   a. v. 19: RESPONSIBILITY CARRIED
      – "He has committed to us the word of reconciliation"
   b. v. 20: REPRESENTING CHRIST
      – "we are ambassadors for Christ"
   c. v. 21: RIGHT CONDITIONING
      – "that we might become the righteousness of God"
B. v. 23: Brotherhood

    As the writer is near the close of this treatise his appeal is based upon the fellowship of discipleship that believers have in connection with Jesus Christ. He shares that Timothy has been set free and that he desire to see his readers in the near future. This appeal has substance because of the spiritual family relationship that Christians have with one another. In Romans 12:1-5 we are given an overview of foundation for our spiritual family. He we see …

1. v. 12:1: Plea of God
   Intro. Request – "I beseech you"
     (1). From a Person – "I [God}"
     (2). Given Powerfully – "beseech"
     (3). to be taken Personally – "you" [individually}
   a. Reason – "therefore" – see Romans 11:36 =
      → "all things are ...
      (1). Plea (text) "of Him"
      (2). Presentation (12:1b) – "through Him"
      (3). Passage (12:2) – "to Him"
      (*). Purpose = "to whom (Christ) be glory forever. Amen"
   b. Requirement – "brethren" – see Romans 11:33-35 =
      (1). v. 33: Salvation is from a Supernatural God
      (2). v. 34: Salvation is from a Sovereign God
      (3). v. 35: Salvation is from a Sympathizing God
   c. Rationale – "by the mercies of God" See Rom11:30-32
      (1). v. 30: Faith – Shared in the Children of Israel
      (2). v. 31: Faith – Seen in Christianity
      (3). v. 32: Faith – Source in Christ's Judgment
          [John 3:18-19: "He that believes on Him is not
          condemned; but he that believes not is
          condemned already, because he has not believed
          in the name of the only begotten Son of God.
          And this is the condemnation, that light is come
          into the world, and men loved darkness rather
          than the light, because their deeds were evil."]
   *. Release to God – "that ye present your bodies ..."
      (1). Resigned to God – "a living sacrifice"
      (2). Righteous as God – "holy"
      (3). Receivable by God – "acceptable"
      (*). Reasonable – "which is your reasonable service"

2. v. 12:2: Passage To God – "but be ye transformed ..."
   a. Rejection of the Sin of Man
      "and be not conformed to this world"
   b. Renewal by the Schooling of the Mind
      "by the renewing of your mind"

    c. Revealing of the Spiritual Message
    "that ye may prove what is that … will of God"
      (1). Sound (moral) – "good"
      (2). Suitable (spiritual) – "acceptable"
      (3). Standard (Christ) – "perfect"
3. v. 12:3-5: Position In God
  Intro. v. 3a: Declaration of Importance
      "For I say, through the grace given unto me, to every man that is among you."
    (1). Spoken Importance – "I say"
    (2). Source of Invitation – "grace"
    (3). Shared Involvement – "every man among you"
  a. v. 3b: Down "to earth" in our Thinking
      "Not to think of himself more highly than he ought to think: but to think soberly, according as God has dealt to every man the measure of faith."
    (1). Honest Thoughts – "soberly"
    (2). Helpful Thoughts – "as God has dealt"
    (3). Heavenly Thoughts – "the measure of faith"
  b. v. 4: Difference In Function
      "For as we have many members in one body, and all members have not the same office"
    →See 1 Corinthians 12:4-6:
    (1). Talented – "diversities of gifts, but the same Spirit"
    (2). Tone-Setters – differences of administration, but the same Lord"
    (3). Trustworthy – "diversities of operations, but the same God"
  c. v. 5: Devotion To One Another
      "so we being many, are on body in Christ, and every one members one of another."
    (1). Ephesians 4:4-6: Connected By Faith
      "There is one body, and one Spirit in the bond of peace, One Lord, one faith, one baptism, one God and Father of all, who is above all, and through all, and in you all."

(2). 1 Peter 3:8: Communicate our Feelings
  "Finally, be ye all of one mind, having compassion one to another, love as brethren, be pitiful, be courteous."
  (3). 1 Corinthians 12:26: Collaborate as a Family
  "and whether one member suffer, all the members suffer with it; or one member be honored, all members rejoice with it."
C. v. 24-25: Conversations

Our writer concludes his treatise by encouraging his readers to be willing to share with their leaders (pastors) and the other church members (the saints) the information that has just been gleaned. The writer also sends greetings from the Christians located in Italy. The writer ends his entire work with the focus on God's grace. In accepting the grace of God and by yielding to Jesus Christ as our Lord we surely are compelled to follow His great Mandate as found in Matthew 28:13-20:

1. v. 18a: Our MOVING
"and Jesus came and spoke to them, saying"
2. v. 18b: Our MOTIVATION
Jesus said: "All authority has been given to Me in heaven and earth."
3. v. 19a: MAKE Disciples
"Go therefore and make disciples of all the nations"
4. v. 19b: MARK Disciples
"baptize them in the name of the Father and of the Son and of the Holy Spirit"
5. v. 20a: MATURE Disciples
"teaching them to observe all things that I have commanded you"
6. v. 20b: The MAGNIFICENCE of The Work
Jesus said: "and lo I am with you always, even to the end of the age."
7. v. 20c: The METHOD of The Work
"Amen" = "So Let It Be" = I will do it Your way!

Made in United States
Cleveland, OH
12 January 2025